Agnes Ayre's NOTEBOOK

Recipes from Old St. John's

Roger Pickavance & Agnes Marion Murphy

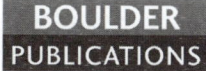
BOULDER PUBLICATIONS

Library and Archives Canada Cataloguing in Publication

Pickavance, Roger, 1943-, author
    Agnes Ayre's notebook : recipes from old St. John's / Roger Pickavance & Agnes Marion Murphy.

ISBN 978-1-77523-459-3 (softcover)

    1. Ayre, Agnes, 1890-1940--Diaries. 2. Cooking, Canadian—Newfoundland and Labrador style. 3. Cookbooks. I. Murphy, Agnes Marion, 1954-, author II. Ayre, Agnes, 1890-1940 . Diaries. Selections. III. Title. IV. Title: Notebook.

TX715.6.P52 2018   641.59718   C2018-905587-1

© 2018 Agnes Marion Murphy and Roger Pickavance

Design and layout: Todd Manning
Editor: Stephanie Porter
Copy editor: Iona Bulgin
Printed in Canada

Excerpts from this publication may be reproduced under licence from Access Copyright, or with the express written permission of Boulder Publications Ltd., or as permitted by law. All rights are otherwise reserved and no part of this publications may be reproduced, stored in a retrieval system, or transmitted in any form or by any means, electronic, mechanical, photocopying, scanning, recording, or otherwise, except as specifically authorized.

We acknowledge the financial support of the Government of Newfoundland and Labrador through the Department of Tourism, Culture and Recreation.

For my Newfoundland sisters.
—Roger Pickavance

For my mother, Janet Cecily Ayre Murphy, 1921-2005
—Agnes Marion Murphy

Acknowledgements

The authors wish to acknowledge the invaluable assistance provided by staff of the Centre for Newfoundland Studies, Queen Elizabeth II Library, Memorial University, St. John's, and in particular we thank Joan Ritcey, former head of the Centre.

We would also like to thank some descendants and relatives of Agnes Ayre: Miller Ayre, Terence Murphy, and Kathleen Knowling, for their generous help.

Table of Contents

Introduction
1

Agnes Marion Miller Ayre
3

The Notebook
9

The Recipes
13

Introduction

Mrs. Agnes Marion Miller Ayre had a remarkable and productive life, albeit a relatively short one of only 50 years. This book is about one small, overlooked aspect of that life, the recipe collection she wrote down in a small notebook starting in 1917. We can be sure of that date because on the front endpaper she has written "Agnes M. Ayre Murray's Pond Aug. 1917," but we don't know if the entire collection was written in that year.

This notebook was inherited by Mrs. Ayre's daughter, Janet C. Ayre, and now belongs to her granddaughter, Agnes Marion Murphy. Mrs. Ayre had a cook and one or two general maids, and it would have been unusual if a comfortable, middle-class family of the day did not have such servants. The family maintains that this recipe collection was compiled largely for the benefit of the cook, plausible given the range and depth of Mrs. Ayre's other activities, which would have left little time for her to spend in the kitchen.

But that cook must have been experienced, because many of the recipes have no directions, and those that do are often skimpy—as in the simple instruction "bake," with no indication of type of vessel, temperature, or time. Few of the recipes have what we would consider these days a minimum set of instructions. Some omit essential ingredients, or are misleading in other ways, which would require a knowledgeable cook to look at a recipe and make allowances.

Few recipes for everyday dishes are included: no boiled dinners, no roast chickens, no fried codfish, and so forth. It was likely assumed that the cook would already have a repertoire of such basics—the notebook provided instruction on slightly out-of-the-ordinary dishes, together with interesting (or at least ingenious) ways of being frugal with leftovers. No doubt the lady of the house, then as now, was suspicious of the supposed wasteful habits of cooks in general.

This notebook is a primary-source historical document, the gold standard of historical research: an original handwritten manuscript by an identified author whose origins, education, and situation in society are known. It offers a snapshot in time of what the lady of a middle-class household in World War I St. John's, Newfoundland, thought worth recording and keeping, and feeding to her family.

But it is not just an historical document. It is also a collection of historical recipes, most of which can be cooked and enjoyed today. Since we both cooked (or tried to cook) all the recipes, we make no apologies for sharing our opinions of some of the recipes. Some methods seem unnecessarily elaborate, but in the interests of historical accuracy we have followed suit, although we point out where steps can be omitted or altered. And many recipes can be speeded up by using modern electrical, kitchen appliances—not historically correct, for sure, but it certainly cuts out a lot of manual labour—after all, who wants to whip egg whites by hand with a balloon whisk?

Although most of the recipes work very well, some do not work at all, or at least did not work for us using 21st-century ingredients. But in all cases, we have retained them to keep the historical record complete.

Agnes Marion Miller Ayre

Agnes Marion Miller was born in St. John's on February 2, 1890, the third child of Lewis Haldane Miller and Mary Peter Morison. She was of Scottish descent on both sides: her father was born in Menstrie, near Stirling, and her mother's grandfather emigrated from Stornoway on the Isle of Lewis in the Outer Hebrides.

Mary and Lewis married in 1883. Their first son, Andrew, was born in 1884. A second son, John, was born 1886 and died from diphtheria in 1889. Agnes was followed in 1892 by another daughter, Janet. Andrew was educated at the Presbyterian College, and while working for Canadian Pacific Railways in Winnipeg, enlisted in the Canadian Expeditionary Forces in 1915. After seeing active service, he died of pneumonia in London in 1917. Both Agnes and Janet were educated at Bishop Spencer College, St. John's, a school for girls which provided a general education. The sisters were bright, lively girls and married cousins Harold and Eric Ayre. These young men were grandsons of Charles Robert Ayre, who was born in 1819 in Exeter, England, emigrated to Newfoundland, and worked as a clerk for Bowring's. In 1846 he went into business with John Steer, and that business eventually became Ayre and Sons, a general merchandise firm.

Agnes married Harold Cecil Ayre on June 10, 1913, at St. Andrew's Presbyterian Church (the Kirk), in St. John's. The best man was Harold's younger brother, Gerald, and both his cousin Eric Ayre (Agnes's sister Janet's fiancé; they married in 1915) and his cousin Wilfrid Ayre attended as ushers. Gerald, Eric, and Wilfred all enlisted in the Newfoundland Regiment, and three years later all were killed on July 1 at Beaumont Hamel on the first day of the battle of the Somme. Another cousin, Bernard Ayre (Eric's brother), enlisted in the Norfolk Regiment, and was also killed the same day. Two other cousins of Harold, Ronald (Royal Flying Corps), and Charles (Newfoundland Regiment) survived the war.

Agnes and Harold were a well-suited couple. They enjoyed card games, reading, rambles in the country with their dogs, and rolling up the carpets to make room for dancing. They loved gardening, and in addition to planting flowers and shrubs, established a small, walled kitchen-garden at their summer house "Treetops" near Murray's Pond, Portugal Cove. They had four children: Lewis Haldane (1914–85),

Agnes M.M. Ayre, daughter Janet and husband Harold Ayre.

Frederick William (1915–86), Andrew Haldane (1917), and Janet Cecily (1921–2005).

When not at Treetops, the family lived at 120 Military Road, St. John's. This home was built after the Great Fire of 1892 in the mansard-roofed, second empire style: three stories and a full basement. The kitchen was in the basement, and Janet recounted[1] dashing home from Bishop Spencer College at recess time to the attractions of the kitchen, where something was always going on, and where there was a barrel of Nova Scotian apples to be sampled. She also mentioned a cook and one or two general domestic servants.[2] A dumb waiter connected the kitchen with the dining area above, typical of houses of this style.

Agnes, an avid reader, accumulated a significant personal library, including a collection of books about Newfoundland—unusual for her day—and was a member of a book club. Her copy of the 1925 *Presbyterian Ladies' Aid Cook Book* is still in the family[3] and she also had a copy of the very first cookbook compiled and published in Newfoundland, the 1905 *Ladies' College Aid Society Cook Book*. She also read periodicals from both the US and England.[4]

Agnes and her family enjoyed the outdoors and picnicked whenever possible. In her own words: "Winter picnics are fun. Summer ones are better. October picnics are best of all. The Fireweed's glowing magenta has turned to heads of cotton and blown away ... Larch and Birch and Dogberry trees are having a last fashion parade, flaunting their lovely golden gowns. To sea, miles of shimmering blue. Inland not a fence, not a dwelling. So free, so clean, so sweet. Bury one's nose in Crowberry cushions ... The heavenly honey smell of it all."[5] The family was proudly patriotic. Newfoundland at that time was a Dominion of Great Britain, in essence an independent country, quite separate from Canada. As Agnes put it:

> Monarch of all we survey, we picnic on a headland and gaze out over our great silvery bays. Below in the coves are little whitewashed cottages, their pocket-handkerchief gardens filled with flowers ... On the beach are wharves, flakes, vats of oil, boats, and ropes. Strangers turn up their fastidious noses. The smell of codfish is too much for them. But Newfoundlanders love it all. The ponds, streams, the barrens, the wild flowers, the white Water Lilies in quiet boggy places, all are free, to be enjoyed by rich and poor alike.[6]

With their mother's encouragement, Agnes and Janet were active in social causes from a young age. Agnes participated in the Women's Patriotic Association and was active in the Newfoundland Outport Nursing and Industrial Association (NONIA, founded 1920), the Red Cross, and fundraising for a new school. She was an active member of the Current Events Club, later re-named the Old Colony Club, which flourished for 25 years from about 1909.[7] The club played a major role in adult female education and provided an incubator for early discussions, debate, and action concerning woman's suffrage; the fight for votes for women in Newfoundland is well documented.[8]

Agnes's lifelong interest in drawing and painting was well established by her teens. In 1906, at the age of 16, she received a full certificate from the Royal Drawing Society (through the local School of Art) for obtaining honours in all seven grades—to that date, the youngest student to have won it.[9] Her daughter Janet recalled that "[a]t every opportunity she could be found, surrounded by a crowd of children, not to mention adults, dogs, and goats, who always came from afar to watch her *skitchin*."[10]

Agnes was a founding member of the Newfoundland Art Society in 1925, a group that enjoyed painting and met regularly to encourage each other.[11] The society organized

1. Maple.
2. Jewelweed.
3. Marestail.
4. Sedge.
5. Pyrola.
6. Bogbean.
7. Moonwort.
8. Loosestrife.
9. Violet.
10. Rhodora.
11. Horsetail.
12. Speedwell.
13. Orchid.
14. Holly.

Newfoundland wildflowers by Agnes M.M. Ayre. From *The Book of Newfoundland*.

local annual art exhibitions, initially to raise funds to support the Old Colony Club. Eventually, the artists sent works to exhibitions in London, Halifax, and Montreal. The society also brought in exhibitions; an exhibit of 50 watercolours from the National Gallery of Canada, Ottawa, at the Royal Stores on Water Street, St. John's, drew considerable attention in 1936.

Mounting all these exhibitions entailed hanging hundreds of paintings on plaster walls without driving any nails. This difficulty led Agnes to exclaim: "Oh, for a permanent room! Oh, for a Newfoundland Art Gallery, where works, now scattered in many parts of the world, by Maurice Cullen, Miss Macpherson, Henry Bradshaw, Mrs. McNeil, Mr. Gosling, Mr. Harris, Mrs. Power and others, could be here for all to enjoy."[12]

Agnes M.M. Ayre out sketching; location unknown.

Agnes's book *Wild Flowers of Newfoundland*, part III,[13] was one volume of a planned four-part monumental but unfinished work that started as a painting exercise in 1927. In her own words: "A friend asked if she might use them as illustrations for a little book she was preparing for the 'Guides.' Collecting two days a week, and painting from six in the morning to six at night all summer, by October I had finished about two hundred and fifty. Eight were as many as I could paint in a day. Then came the task of trying to name them. My friend borrowed three large volumes from Queen's College Library and we spent a day comparing my paintings with the coloured illustrations, but found nothing to resemble them."[14]

Her attempts at identification involved travel to the South Kensington Museum (London), McGill University, and finally to Professor Fernald at the Gray Herbarium, Harvard. A digitized collection of Agnes's botanical painting is available online through the Centre for Newfoundland Studies,[15] Memorial University of Newfoundland's QEII Library. Part of her collection of pressed plants is now in the Memorial University Herbarium, which is named in her honour.

Agnes Marion Miller Ayre died of cancer in June 1940 in St. John's.

The Notebook

The recipes were written in an unremarkable notebook (6 5/8 x 8 7/8 inches), hardbound in black cloth with a maroon spine. Excluding the endpapers, there were originally 50 leaves (100 one-page sides). The pages are not numbered. Each side of each leaf (but not the endpapers) has 23 faint grey-blue printed lines. In its present state, the back cover is missing, with only a fragment of its lining paper remaining, but both endpapers are intact. Nine of the original 50 leaves have been torn out, but strangely enough—and fortunately for us—the pages were torn out before the recipes were written.

The handwriting is that of an educated woman accustomed to writing. The writing style is uniform throughout (except for the last recipe, see below), but the size of the letters and the strength of the pen-strokes change occasionally, so it is likely that she used different pens at different times. She used a variety of blue and black inks.

Some entries have faded much more than others, which is not solely due to sunlight, because if that was the case then whole pages would be faded, and there are many cases of differential fading on the same page. For example, the page with recipes 98 and 99 on it, number 98 has faded considerably, while number 99 is still dark and pronounced.

Mrs. Ayre evidently wrote many of the recipes down quickly, omitting definite articles and conjunctions, and plays fast and loose with punctuation and other such impediments to rapid transcription. Many recipes simply have spaces between words where one might expect a conjunction and/or some punctuation. Her spelling is uniformly good with occasional notable exceptions, such as *mayonaise* and *cinamon*. Her grammar is indicative of a good education but is completely subservient to the needs of writing quickly.

With the one exception mentioned below, none of the marginalia appear to be in Mrs. Ayre's hand. On the inside of the front cover "Amon," the name "Mrs. Harold C. Ayre," and a few indecipherable squiggles are pencilled in. On the recto of the front endpaper are indecipherable marks top right, the isolated word "Miss," the isolated word "Ayre," and the name "Mr. Lewis Ayre" (her son). Between her numbered list of recipes on pages 1 to 4 and the first recipe on page 9, she had left pages 5 to 8 blank. Someone else has written in pencil a recipe for dark cake on page 6 and a recipe for marble cake on page 7. Since these two recipes are of unknown provenance, they are not included in this book.

Superimposed on the bottom of recipe 92 is a sketch of a human face, possibly in Mrs. Ayre's hand, which would fit with her known artistic ability. "Ayre & Sons" is written along the left-hand margin and at 90 degrees to the text of recipe 93. Written on top of and parallel with the first line of recipe 93 are the numerals 1 2 3 4 5 6 7 8 9 0, in a child's hand. In the top margin of page 11 someone, possibly Mrs. Ayre, has written "pour & power" at 45 degrees to the text. On the recto of the back endpaper is a short, three-line untitled recipe in ink, and a recipe for salad dressing in pencil, neither in her hand. And on the verso of the back endpaper is a recipe for homemade ginger ale, in pencil, not in her hand. As these are of unknown provenance they are not included.

Considered marginalia for present purposes are some items tucked into the notebook: three newspaper clippings of recipes, a small card with a recipe from the Royal Baking Powder Company, three variously sized sheets of notepaper with recipes scribbled on them (but none in her hand), and a small booklet of recipes using yeast from the Fleischmann Company dated 1907. There is also a small envelope containing a single

92 Delicious pudding –

1 breakfast cup breadcrumbs ½ lb either prunes, (soaked & chopped) or raisins or dates – 2 tablesp tapioca soaked in milk or water all night – 2 table brown s 2 tablesp butter or dripping – ½ teasp soda – Steam 2½ hours

93 Parkin – 2 lbs oatmeal ½ lb brown sugar 6 oz dripping. 1 oz best ground ginger crumble all together mix to stiff dough with little molasses – Roll out – cut into squares & bake on a tin in a quick oven 15 to 20 mins –

94 Dainty pudding (economical)
Put into a basin a heaped teacup flour pinch salt 1 tablesp sugar 1½ oz margarine or butter mix all well together and add a tablesp jam, lastly add teasp soda dissolved in ¼ tea cup warm water stir well put in a well greased

sheet of paper with a recipe for Rich Christmas Pudding, but not in her hand. Although some of these are interesting recipes, they are not included in this book.

The notebook recipes are in no particular order, and certainly not arranged according to topic, so we assume Mrs. Ayre simply wrote them down as she came across them. A numbered list of recipes appears on the first four pages, but they are simply listed in the order they appear in the notebook, so the reader still has to plow through the list to find anything.

On the list of contents on the first four pages, the recipe numbers go to 140, but there are in fact 142 recipes, because there are two number 7s and two number 68s. Some recipes are really several in one, as in Dandelions (28), which covers a cooked vegetable, a soup, and two salads. Others are in two separate recipes but are really parts of the same recipe. For example, 37 and 38 are a marshmallow cake and its icing separated into two different numbers. In only one instance is a recipe illustrated: Orange Jelly (47) has two small pen-and-ink sketches that clarify the instruction to serve the jelly "in orange baskets or half orange skins cut into points."

Sources of most of the recipes are obscure. Mrs. Ayre presumably had cookbooks, but we can be certain of only one that was published before 1917, the 1905 L.C.A.S. cookbook.[1] This was the first locally compiled cookbook, and we know she had a copy because some of her recipes are condensed versions of those in the cookbook, and one in particular (105, Kiffins) is a more or less direct transcription of Kyffins on page 78 of the L.C.A.S. cookbook, including the unusual measurement "a plate of flour." We know she later acquired a copy of the 1925 P.L.A. cookbook.[2]

Mrs. Ayre read both US and English periodicals, which, together with newspapers, were often sources of recipes. Some advertisers exhorted women to write in for a free booklet of recipes, and Mrs. Ayre obliged—the Fleischmann's booklet referred to above was an example. Other advertisers both offered booklets and printed recipes directly in their advertisements. The Royal Baking Powder Company, for example, not only offered a "booklet of recipes which economize in eggs and other expensive ingredients mailed free" but also printed recipes directly in their advertisements. And from one of them, Mrs. Ayre copied her recipe for Chocolate Sponge Roll (33) verbatim.

Other recipe sources must have been friends, relatives, and others of her social circle. Some of these are acknowledged in titles, such as Moll's Cake (116), Carrie's Chocolate Cake (117), and Chowder Mrs. H. (134). We are uncertain who Carrie was, but Moll and Mrs. H. were the same person, Mrs. Moll Herder.[3] We hope that serendipity will bring to light more of Mrs. Ayre's sources.

The Recipes

The recipes appear here in the same order as in Mrs. Ayre's notebook. Each starts with a transcription, in italics, of her entry. The transcription is as accurate as possible, including her spelling, punctuation, capitalization, abbreviations, and line breaks. The only deliberate change is to justify each line of her recipe to the left, rather than copying the random indentations of the original, and to omit her page breaks.

We had to make judgment calls in many places, such as interpretations of her liberal use of the dash—sometimes used in place of a period, sometimes separating phrases where a conjunction might be expected, and sometimes where a dash does indeed seem appropriate. Rarely, we made assumptions about what she had written where the original was torn or obscured. These are indicated in square brackets.

We have cooked all of Mrs. Ayre's recipes, many several times, in order to sort out mistakes and ambiguities. After each transcribed original recipe are our notes about that recipe, including commentary about ingredients and methods, mistakes, necessary corrections, and minor improvements. We have not attempted to completely revise the recipes to make them suitable for modern tastes—the recipes must speak for themselves, albeit with some interpretation and judicious tweaking. Finally, we present each recipe in the way we cooked it, in a more approachable form suited for today's cooks.

Many of the measurements Mrs. Ayre used are confusing for today's cooks. For example, in North America these days the mainstream seems to be that weight is only used for bulk items—4 pounds of apples, but seldom 1 ounce of butter—while all smaller quantities of ingredients, whether solid or liquid, are in cups and spoons: 2 tablespoons of butter, 1 cup of sugar, or 1 cup of milk, for example. Mrs. Ayre also uses some old-fashioned measures such as breakfast cup or dessertspoon, which have fallen out of use. In our versions of her recipes we have converted all her smaller quantities, and all her obsolete, non-standard measures, into volumes (cups and spoons), retained imperial weights only for larger quantities, and in the metric conversions have expressed all solids in grams and all liquids in millilitres.

Mrs. Ayre probably used both American and imperial measures. There was a large British influence in the Newfoundland of her day, but at the same time there were plenty of connections with Canada and the US. It makes no difference to her recipes which measures are used, so we have expressed them in standard US measures, set out below with approximate metric equivalents. Measures are level to the rim of spoon or cup.

1 pound (= 16 oz = 450 g)	1 gallon (= 4 quarts = 3.8 l)	1 tablespoon (= 15 ml)
1 ounce (= 30 g)	1 quart (= 4 cups = 1 l)	1 teaspoon (= 5 ml)
	1 pint (= 2 cups = 500 ml)	½ teaspoon (= 2.5 ml)
	1 cup (= 250 ml)	¼ teaspoon (= 1.3 ml)

Mrs. Ayre frequently specifies a pinch of this or a dash of that, and although subjective and difficult to define, these terms are still widespread. A pinch is usually considered the amount of some powdery substance easily grasped between the tips of forefinger and thumb, but what is a dash? Here we take a dash to be two pinches. But for the sake of consistency, although not of practicality, we have quantified our pinch and our dash below. But even if you have the technology, there is little point in weighing out such tiny portions—better to simply, well, take a pinch or two.

1 dash (= 2 pinches = 1/16 tsp = 0.2 g)	1 pinch (= 1/32 tsp = 0.1 g)

When baking, Mrs. Ayre rarely quotes a temperature in degrees Fahrenheit (and when she does, she is likely copying a recipe from somewhere), but more usually simply mentions a slow, medium, or hot oven. These have all been converted into degrees Fahrenheit in the text, and Celsius equivalents are given here.

176°F = 80°C (custard-setting temperature)
200°F = 95°C
220°F = 105°C
250°F = 120°C
325°F = 165°C
350°F = 180°C

360°F = 180°C (deep-frying temperature)
375°F = 190°C
400°F = 200°C
425°F = 220°C
450°F = 235°C

Temperature equivalents of stages of boiled sugar mentioned in the text:

Thread stage = 230°F/110°C
Soft-ball stage = 240°F/116°C
Hard-ball stage = 260°F/126°C

Soft-crack stage = 276°F/134°C
Hard-crack stage = 302°F/149°C

Unless specified to the contrary: flour is all-purpose white flour; sugar is granulated white sugar; brown sugar is either light or dark brown; salt is finely granular, iodized table salt; molasses is light or "Fancy" grade, not blackstrap; eggs are standard large of North America, about 60 grams (2.1 oz), which approximates to the medium egg of the UK and Europe; milk is whole milk, about 3.25% milk fat, although all recipes work with 1% or 2% milk; cream is 35% milk fat, often sold as whipping cream; butter is salted; crackers are Purity cream crackers, about 2.5 by 2.5 inches (6.5 x 6.5 cm; 10 g each); lard is commercial supermarket grade; pepper is ground black pepper; ginger is dry, ground powder; all spices are ground; cocoa is Fry's; and vanilla is the extract of vanilla beans.

The Recipes

1. Oatmeal cookies.

1 cup sugar
½ " butter
1½ " oatmeal
1 teaspoon b. powder
salt
(1 egg an improvement)
enough milk to mix.

Presumably no instructions were needed because cookies were so familiar. The added egg is an improvement, but the with-egg version needs different treatment from the no-egg style. The no-egg batter spreads out very thinly when baked, whereas with-egg batter spreads far less; two methods are given below. Cookie size can be adjusted to individual taste, but we suggest sizes that work.

Mrs. Ayre no doubt used a well-seasoned baking sheet, lightly greased, providing an essentially non-stick surface. That technique works if the baking sheets are old and well used, but if in doubt use parchment paper (or better, silicone mats) laid on baking sheets, or non-stick baking sheets. Be careful when baking these; they burn easily.

OATMEAL COOKIES
makes 24 or 64 cookies

1 cup (200 g) sugar
½ cup (110 g) butter
1 egg (optional)
1½ cups (225 g) oatmeal

1 teaspoon (5 g) baking powder
⅛ teaspoon (0.8 g) salt
2–3 tablespoons (30–45 ml) milk if not using an egg; no milk if using an egg

Cream together the butter and sugar until pale and fluffy. If using an egg, beat it in. Mix the oatmeal, salt, and baking powder, and stir into the butter mixture.

If you are not using an egg, add 2 tablespoons of milk and mix well. If necessary, add teaspoons more until the loose dough just holds together. Turn out the dough onto a lightly floured surface and roll it into a long cylinder, then either:

Dough with an egg

To make 24 thin, 4-inch-diameter cookies: Divide the dough into 24 portions. Roll each into a ball between your palms, place on a baking sheet, and press into a 2-inch disk. To allow for spreading, centres should be at least 4 inches apart. Bake at 350°F about 12 minutes, or until nicely browned.

Dough without egg

To make about 64 very thin, 3-inch-diameter cookies: Divide the dough into about 64 portions, each about the size of a large grape. Place on a baking sheet and flatten slightly into a disk. Centres should be at least 3 inches apart to allow for spreading. Bake at 350°F for about 10 minutes, or until nicely browned.

2. Bran Bread

3 cups flour
¾ "   bran
1 teasp. bread soda
2 "   cream tartar
1 "   sugar
1 "   salt
Milk or milk and water to mix just soft enough to handle. Bake in covered bake pot about 1 hour.

Although not named as such, this is soda bread, where the cream of tartar takes the place of sour milk (or buttermilk) to provide the acidity which makes the bread soda release carbon dioxide to leaven the bread. The bran was likely wheat bran, the most common of the brans. Oat bran or wheat germ may be used instead. This recipe makes a pleasantly dense-textured bread, which is good the day it is baked, and as good (or better) toasted when a day or two old. Bake in a cast-iron bake pot or a heavy ceramic dish.

This is probably derived from an older recipe, because before the middle of the 19th century soda bread was usually baked in a cast-iron bake pot over an open fire. When domestic ovens became widespread in the kitchens of Newfoundland in the second half of the 19th century, the bake pot was simply put in the oven instead of suspended over the flames.

BRAN BREAD
makes one loaf

3 cups (450 g) flour
¾ cup (85 g) wheat bran
1 teaspoon (5 g) baking soda
2 teaspoons (10 g) cream of tartar
1 teaspoon (4 g) sugar
1 teaspoon (6.5 g) salt
1½ cups (375 ml) milk or equal parts milk and water

Preheat the oven to 400°F. Grease a 2-quart bake pot or similar dish. Mix all the dry ingredients well. Gradually mix in the milk (or milk and water) to make a loose dough. Turn out onto a floured surface and with floured hands gather into a loose ball. Roughly shape into a round or oval that approximates the shape of the baking dish and place it in the dish. The dough does not have to fill the dish completely because it will expand and make itself fit. Cover and bake for about 1 hour.

3. Canada's war cake

(eggless, butterless, milkless)
2 cups brown sugar
2 cups hot water
2 tablespoons lard
1 pk. seedless raisins
1 teasp. salt
1 teasp. cinnamon
1 teasp. cloves
Boil all these ingredients for
5 minutes after they begin to
bubble. When cold add
3 cups flour 1 teaspoon soda dissolved in
1 teasp hot water
Bake in 2 loaves 45 minutes (slow)

War cakes were all the rage in Newfoundland during World War I, and many recipes came from Canada, hence Mrs. Ayre's title. But what was the purpose of a war cake? One official reason given by the Newfoundland Food Control Board was to encourage the use of flour substitutes, to release more flour for the use of the Allies. Mrs. Ayre used regular white flour, however, not substitutes. Nonetheless, a cake with no eggs, butter, or milk kept much longer than other cakes, so could be sent to young men overseas—a far better reason for this style of cake.

How big was that packet of raisins? In Mrs. Ayre's day the pound was the standard unit of weight, so one packet was probably either 1 pound or ½ pound of raisins. After trying this recipe with both amounts, a ½-pound packet (roughly 2 cups of raisins) seems more likely. It is not necessary to mix the soda with water but doing so helps ensure that the soda is completely broken up.

Since Mrs. Ayre specified baking this as loaves, we used greased bread pans, but the recipe works equally well in a round cake pan—a standard 5 by 10-inch loaf pan is the same area as an 8-inch round cake pan. Baking this in two pans, as the original recipe calls for, produces two rather flat loaves, at most 2 inches high. If the recipe is simply baked as one loaf (or cake), it makes a perfectly respectable 4-inch-high cake. For two cakes, double the recipe.

CANADA'S WAR CAKE
makes one 8-inch (20 cm) round cake or one 5 by 10-inch (12.5 by 25 cm) loaf
eggless, butterless, milkless

- 2 cups (500 ml) water
- 2 cups (300 g) brown sugar
- 2 tablespoons (25 g) lard
- 2 cups (300 g) raisins
- 1 teaspoon (6.5 g) salt
- 1 teaspoon (3 g) cloves
- 1 teaspoon (3 g) cinnamon
- 3 cups (450 g) flour
- 1 teaspoon (5 g) baking soda
- 1 teaspoon (5 ml) warm water

Preheat the oven to 350°F. Grease and flour a 5 by 10-inch loaf pan or an 8-inch round cake pan. Put the water, brown sugar, lard, raisins, salt, and spices in a small saucepan, bring to a boil, and simmer for 5 minutes. Leave to cool. Stir the baking soda into 1 teaspoon of warm water, and stir this and the flour into the cooled mixture. Pour and scrape the batter into the prepared pan and bake about 45 minutes, or until a small skewer inserted into the thickest part comes out clean.

3. Canada's war cake
   (eggless, butterless, milkless)
   2 cups brown sugar
   2 cups hot water
   2 tablespoon lard
   1 pk. seedless raisins
   1 teasp. salt
   1 teasp. cinnamon
   1 teasp cloves
   Boil all these ingredients for 5 minutes after they begin to bubble. When cold add
   3 cups flour
   1 teaspoon soda dissolved in
   1 teasp hot water
   Bake in 2 loaves 45 minutes (slow)

4. A perfect loaf of bread.
   6 cups bread flour
   2 cups luke warm water
   1 cake compressed yeast
   2 tablespoons of shortening
   2 tablespoons sugar (1½ teasp salt

4. A perfect loaf of bread

6 cups bread flour
2 cups lukewarm water
1 cake compressed yeast
2 tablespoons of shortening
2 tablespoons sugar (1½ teasp salt.
Pour the lukewarm water into a bowl. add the sugar, salt & fat. Mix the yeast with a little lukewarm water & add to the bowl. Sift in the flour mix the dough until stiff enough to handle, turn out on a slightly floured board and knead the dough until it is soft & elastic. Replace it in the bowl, carefully moisten the top, cover and keep in a warm place – 76 to 80 degrees fahrenheit – for about 2 hours, or until the dough has doubled in bulk. Then knead the dough until it responds quickly when pressed with the finger; divide into 2 loaves, place in baking pans & let rise again in a warm place for half an hour or until again doubled in bulk, bake in a moderate oven 360 – 400 degrees f. – for 60 minutes

Mrs. Ayre puts the kneaded dough back in the mixing bowl, but it is better to use a separate, greased bowl. Rather than moisten the dough and cover with a cloth, omit the moistening and cover the bowl of dough with plastic film.

Unusually, Mrs. Ayre specifies temperatures in this recipe: 76° to 80°F (about 25°C) for the initial rising of the dough, warm even by today's standards. However, the dough will rise perfectly well at any room temperature, but give it more time if the room is on the cool side.

Whether this is a perfect loaf of bread is up for debate. This bread has little to recommend it except when fresh from the oven and liberally anointed with butter and jam. But this style of bread is what most Newfoundlanders think of as "homemade" bread.

A PERFECT LOAF OF BREAD
makes 2 loaves

2 cups (500 ml) lukewarm water
2 tablespoons (25 g) sugar
1½ teaspoons (10 g) salt
1 tablespoon (11 g) dry granular yeast
2 tablespoons (25 g) shortening
6 cups (900 g) flour

Preheat the oven to 400°F. Put the lukewarm water in a bowl and stir in the sugar and salt until dissolved. Sprinkle the yeast over this solution and leave for 5 or 10 minutes until starting to foam. Add the shortening and about 4 cups of flour and stir to make a stiff dough. Turn out onto a floured surface and knead for about 10 minutes, incorporating as much of the remaining 2 cups of flour as possible. Put this ball of dough into a lightly greased bowl, cover with plastic film, and leave in a warm place to rise for 1 to 2 hours, or until it has clearly risen and about doubled in size.

Lightly grease 2 standard loaf pans (5 x 10 inches). Turn the dough out onto a lightly floured surface and knead for about 15 seconds until the dough becomes elastic. Divide into two equal portions, shape each into roughly the shape of the bread pan, turn the ragged edges underneath, and put in the pans. Leave in a warm place for an hour or more, or until the dough has risen above the rim of the pan but has not yet bulged over the edge. Bake for about 60 minutes, or until the bread is well browned. Turn loaves out on a rack to cool.

5. Swedish sponge cake

Beat separately the whites & yolks of 4 eggs. Beat 1 cup of sugar into the yolks, then add ½ cup potato flour, sifted with ¾ teasp cream tartar & ¼ salt. Add lastly 2 teasp lemon & whites of eggs. Bake in a mod. oven 40 minutes.

The ½ cup of potato flour sets the mixture like concrete, making it impossible to fold in the egg whites to make a cake batter. Was potato flour different back then, or was this a mistake? Experimentation showed that only about 2 tablespoons of modern potato flour are needed to thicken the yolk-sugar mixture to the point where whites will fold in easily.

Cream of tartar is normally whipped with egg whites to stabilize them, so the value of mixing tartar with the yolk-sugar mixture is dubious—insofar as this recipe works at all, it works just as well without the tartar.

This makes a rather flat, deflated sponge cake. The potato flour does nothing for the flavour—it makes the cake taste, well, like potatoes, and not in a good way. As with many recipes of the period, this is a bit too sweet for modern tastes.

SWEDISH SPONGE CAKE
makes one 8-inch (20 cm) cake

4 eggs, separated
1 cup (200 g) sugar
2 tablespoons (20 g) potato flour

¾ teaspoon (3 g) cream of tartar
¼ teaspoon (1.5 g) salt
2 teaspoons (10 ml) lemon essence

Preheat the oven to 350°F. Grease and flour an 8-inch round cake pan. Beat the yolks and sugar together until well combined. Mix the potato flour, cream of tartar, and salt well and mix this into the yolk-sugar mixture. Add the lemon essence. Whip the egg whites to soft peaks and immediately fold them into the batter. Pour and scrape this into the prepared cake pan and bake about 35 minutes, or until a small skewer comes out clean.

6. Plain cake

Cream together ½ cup butter & 1 cup sugar add one at a time 2 eggs & 1 teasp. lemon, sift together 1 cup potato flour 1 cup flour 1 teasp. baking powder & a pinch salt. Add this alternately with 3 tablesps water to creamed mixture and bake in moderately quick oven.

Mrs. Ayre's recipe calls for 1 cup of potato flour, but as in the Swedish sponge cake, this is too much; it is difficult to tell whether this was a mistake or if potato flour was different 100 years ago. This recipe is too sweet for many tastes.

PLAIN CAKE
makes one 8-inch (20 cm) cake

1 cup (200 g) sugar
½ cup (110 g) butter
2 eggs
1 teaspoon (5 ml) lemon essence

¼ cup (40 g) potato flour
1 teaspoon (5 g) baking powder
⅛ teaspoon (0.8 g) salt
3 tablespoons (45 ml) water

Preheat the oven to 350°F. Grease and flour an 8-inch round cake pan. Cream together the sugar and butter until fluffy and pale yellow. Beat in the eggs one at a time, then beat in the salt and lemon essence. Mix the flour, potato flour, and baking powder and beat them into the butter-egg batter along with 3 tablespoons of water. Scrape into the prepared pan and smooth the top. Bake for about 40 minutes, or until a small skewer inserted in the thickest part comes out clean.

7. Mayonaise

4 eggs (2 hard boiled & 2 uncooked)
½ teasp ground mustard
¼ teasp red pepper
salt to taste
1½ tablespoons strong vinegar
Beat well yolks of raw eggs & add olive oil a teasp at a time beating with fork until eggs are stiffened. Then smooth with yolks of cooked eggs mustard & pepper add enough oil to make smooth paste. Mix the two by degrees & thin with vinegar.

This can be made by beating with a fork, but a small whisk is easier. Either way, make sure the oil and raw yolks are at a warm room temperature.

How much olive oil is not specified, but to get the egg yolks "stiffened" at least ¾ cup is required. But in fact those 2 raw yolks will carry up to 2 cups of oil. She says to add the oil 1 teaspoon at a time, but it is much better initially to add smaller amounts, about ½ teaspoon, until about 3 tablespoons have been added and an emulsion is forming.

Rather than simply mash the hard-boiled yolks in a bowl, they can be rubbed through a fine sieve, which will ensure that no small lumps of yolk remain. For the red pepper, use cayenne pepper. As the quality of most ground mustard powder is dubious, use 1 teaspoon of prepared Dijon mustard instead. Makes an unconventional but excellent mayonnaise.

MAYONNAISE
makes about 1¼ cups (300 ml) mayonnaise

- **2 raw egg yolks**
- **2 hard-boiled egg yolks**
- **¾ cup (200 ml) or more olive oil**
- **2 tablespoons (30 ml) olive oil**
- **½ teaspoon (1.5 g) ground mustard**
- **¼ teaspoon (0.75 g) red pepper**
- **½ teaspoon (3.3 g) salt, or more to taste**
- **1½ tablespoons (23 ml) vinegar**

Whisk the raw egg yolks, then whisk in ¾ cup of olive oil—begin by adding it slowly, drop by drop. Mash the hard-boiled yolks with the mustard, salt, cayenne pepper, and about 2 tablespoons of olive oil, or just enough to make a smooth paste. Whisk the hard-boiled yolk mixture into the raw yolk and oil. Then whisk in 1 tablespoon of vinegar, and add more to achieve the desired texture.

FRESH EGGS.

For Sale by Clift, Wood & Co.,
26 Cases Fresh P. E. Island Corn-fed Eggs,
just arrived, ex Volunteer.

Evening Telegram, March 22, 1890.

7 (b) Sauce for green salads

Place tablesp lime juice in a bowl add tablesp celery salt, a saltspoon pepper and dash cayenne. Mix in a little at a time alternately 3 tablesp oil and 2 lime juice. Stir rapidly so ingredients will mix smoothly add tablesp – finely cut chives

If that 1 tablespoon of lime juice initially mixed with the celery salt is in addition to the 2 tablespoons mentioned farther down, then the sauce becomes excessively acidic—2 tablespoons in total seem a better idea. Whether 2 or 3 tablespoons are used, the mixture does not form a stable emulsion, so whisk it well just before using.

What sort of lime juice Mrs. Ayre was using is not certain. Fresh limes were available, but rare—certainly not as common as fresh lemons. More likely she used bottled lime juice. Rose's brand was in the stores, probably the unsweetened variety, as opposed to the sweetened lime cordial that is more common today. This recipe has been tested with real lime juice, with Rose's lightly sweetened lime cordial, and with standard unsweetened bottled lime juice made from concentrate. Any of these will make a dressing, but only freshly squeezed lime juice is actually pleasant.

The celery salt is a highly variable ingredient. These combinations of salt and ground celery seed vary in both the quality of the celery component and the proportion of salt. We used an off-the-shelf supermarket brand to test this recipe.

Saltspoons were tiny spoons for taking salt from a small dish to a plate, to be either sprinkled on the food or piled on the rim of the plate and dipped into as liked. Sizes varied, but ¼ teaspoon was an average.

This dressing needs to be made with freshly squeezed lime juice. Overall, it has no advantage over a simple vinaigrette.

SAUCE FOR GREEN SALADS
makes about ½ cup (15 ml) sauce

1 tablespoon (20 g) celery salt
¼ teaspoon (0.75 g) pepper
dash (0.25 g) cayenne pepper

2 tablespoons (30 ml) freshly squeezed lime juice
3 tablespoons (45 ml) oil
1 tablespoon (4 g) finely chopped chives

Mix the celery salt, pepper, and cayenne with about 1 tablespoon of lime juice to make a loose paste. Whisk in the rest of the lime juice and the olive oil alternately to make an emulsion. Quickly stir in the chives if using them, and use the dressing immediately.

8. Gingerbread

1 cup molasses
butter size of an egg
2 teasp ginger
1 teasp soda dissolved in
½ cup boiling water
flour to thicken.

Butter the size of an egg approximates to ¼ cup. Dissolving the baking soda in water is a useful way of ensuring no lumps but is not essential if you mash it well with the flour. If you do mix it with water, boiling water is unnecessary—simply use cold or warm water and stir well to make sure the soda is completely broken up.

This makes a pleasant, rather dense cake, rich with molasses but not overpowered by it.

GINGERBREAD
makes one 8-inch (20 cm) cake

1 cup (250 ml) molasses
¼ cup (50 g) butter
2 teaspoons (6 g) ground ginger
1 teaspoon (5 g) baking soda
½ cup (125 ml) warm water
2½ cups (375 g) flour

Preheat the oven to 350°F. Butter and flour an 8-inch round cake pan. Mix the molasses, butter, and ginger well. Dissolve the baking soda in the warm water. Mix the flour and the dissolved soda into the molasses mixture, then pour and scrape it into the prepared cake pan. Bake for 35 or 40 minutes, or until a small skewer stuck in the thickest part of the cake comes out clean.

> *9. Gingerbread*
>
> 1 lb flour
> ¼ lb butter & lard
> 1 tablespoon ginger
> 1 teasp soda dissolved in
> 3 tablespoons milk
> 1 pint molasses
> Heat in a moderate oven –
> Cook

This cake always sinks in the middle, and there is too much molasses in proportion to everything else. For an old-fashioned molasses-ginger cake, try the previous recipe.

GINGERBREAD

makes one 8-inch (20 cm) cake

2 cups (500 ml) molasses
½ cup (110 g total) butter and lard mixed, about equal parts
1 tablespoon (9 g) ground ginger
3 cups (450 g) flour
1 teaspoon (5 g) baking soda
3 tablespoons (45 ml) milk

Preheat the oven to 350°F. Butter and flour a deep 8-inch round cake pan. Mix the molasses, butter and lard, and ginger well. Dissolve the baking soda in the milk, then mix this and the flour into the molasses mixture to make a smooth batter. Pour and scrape into the prepared cake pan and bake for 60 minutes, or until a small skewer stuck into the cake comes out clean.

10. Marmalade (Grape fruit)

1 grape fruit
1 orange
4 lbs sugar
1 lemon
3 quarts water
Slice fruit as fine as possible
Remove seeds & cut from grapefruit the centre pith. Place fruit in bowl. Cover with water & allow to stand for 24 hours. Simmer 1½ hours. Allow mixture to stand overnight. Next day bring to boiling point. Add sugar and allow to boil slowly until fruit *is* clear.
If pips and pith are boiled in a little water which added gives a rather bitter taste.

The technique of long soaking and/or preliminary boiling was in vogue in 19th- and early 20th-century marmalade-making. Mrs. Beeton, for example, in one of her marmalade recipes in her *Book of Household Management* (1861), advocates boiling the orange rinds for 2 hours, changing the water three times, to remove bitterness from the rind. This is likely totally unnecessary then or now, but in the interests of historical accuracy we followed suit.

Mrs. Ayre's recommendation to boil until the fruit is clear (translucent) is not reliable—the fruit goes translucent way before the setting point is reached. At the beginning of the 20th century the blob-on-a-cold-plate technique was well known (see any standard work on jam-making), so we are surprised that she does not mention this. Using a thermometer is a better method.

Unlike in Mrs. Ayre's day, most oranges and grapefruit in the early 21st century have few seeds, so there is little point saving them. But for Seville oranges, for example, where three dozen or more large pits can be found in a single orange, it's worth saving them and stewing them separately in a little water as she recommends for her grapefruit pits. Add the stewing water to the main batch.

Even for those heavily prejudiced in favour of Seville oranges, this is a surprisingly good marmalade. There is more jellied matrix in proportion to the fruit than usual, but for some that is a bonus. This recipe makes enough to fill about six 2-cup Mason jars to the shoulder.

MARMALADE (GRAPEFRUIT)
makes 10 cups (2.5 l)

1 whole (about 1 lb/500 g) grapefruit
1 whole (about 8 oz/250 g) orange
1 whole (about 6 oz/175 g) lemon
3 quarts (3 l) water
4 pounds (1.8 kg) sugar

Cut all fruit in quarters lengthways. If there is a large tube of pith in the centre of the grapefruit, cut it out. Remove any visible seeds. Sliver as thinly as possible across each quarter, removing any seeds. Mix the sliced fruit and the water and let stand for 24 hours. Then bring it to a boil and simmer 1½ hours, then let stand overnight. Next day bring the mixture back to a boil and add the sugar. Boil gently until the setting point is reached.

AYRE & SONS, LTD., Grocery Department

Received by S. S. Florizel

Bananas,   Grape Fruit,   Turnips, Carrots,
Oranges,   Plums, Apples,   Cabbage,
Cherries, Beet,   Cucumbers,   New York Beef.

Evening Telegram, July 19, 1912.

11. Fruit fudge

Boil 3 cups gran sugar
3 teasp cocoa
¾ cup milk
1 tablesp butter. When it forms a soft ball in cold water add ½ cup each of ch. raisins, nuts, ¼ cup cocoanut ¾ figs. Pour into buttered pan. Stuff dates.

Because cocoa powder tends to clump, it was likely sifted through a fine sieve; in general, this is a wise precaution. Cocoanut was desiccated, shredded coconut. The larger the date, the easier to stuff; use a Medjool date or similar, those with the pits still in, so the cavity makes a convenient receptacle for a portion of fudge. Those who find fudge excruciatingly sweet will not be converted by this recipe. But those that are fond of fudge will find it very much to their taste.

FRUIT FUDGE
makes about 65 stuffed dates

3 cups (600 g) sugar
¾ cup (190 ml) milk
1 tablespoon (7.5 g) cocoa
1 tablespoon (15 g) butter

½ cup (75 g) raisins
½ cup (60 g) chopped nuts
¾ cup (100 g) chopped figs
¼ cup (20 g) desiccated coconut
60–70 large dates

Butter a shallow 8-inch square pan (the butter helps keep the mixture from sticking). Cut the raisins in halves. Chop the nuts and figs to pieces no bigger than the raisins. Sift the cocoa through a fine sieve to break up any small lumps. Boil the sugar, milk, butter, and cocoa to the soft-ball stage. Add the chopped raisins, nuts, and figs. Add the coconut, mix well, and then scrape into the pan. Before the mixture is completely cool, and while it is still malleable, stuff the dates. Slit the dates along one side, pop out the pit, then fill the pit cavity with fruit fudge. This recipe will fill about 60–70 large dates, or more smaller ones.

> *Add pineapple to following or figs or chopped walnuts*
>
> ## 12) Cream Candy.
>
> *Put 1 sm. Tablespoon butter in pan to melt. Add 2 cups sugar (moist brown) and ⅓ cup milk. Stir till dissolved & then boil 4 or 5 minutes till candy. Flavour when off stove. When cooling beat*

Mrs. Ayre's instruction to boil the sugar and milk for "4 or 5 minutes till candy" is confusing. After only 5 minutes the sugar and milk will at most be at the soft-ball stage and if taken off the heat at this point ends up like fudge rather than candy, particularly if you follow her instruction to beat while cooling. If boiled for about 15 minutes, it reaches the soft-crack stage, when it will set to a more candy-like consistency. But if beaten as it cools, it will end up coarsely crystalline, again more fudge-like than candy. Either way, add the flavouring and chopped nuts (or figs or pineapple) after removing it from the heat.

Mrs. Ayre does not specify the flavouring, so we used vanilla, but lemon essence also works. Although fresh pineapples were occasionally advertised in her day, she probably used canned pineapple because it was commonly available and is specified in other recipes (e.g., recipe 43), and that is what we used when trying this recipe.

CREAM CANDY
makes about 24 portions

2 cups (350 g) brown sugar
⅓ cup (85 ml) milk
1 tablespoon (15 g) butter
1 teaspoon (5 ml) vanilla

⅓ cup (40 g) coarsely chopped walnuts
or similar amounts of chopped figs
or pineapple

Bring the sugar, milk, and butter to a bubbling simmer. Simmer about 10 to 15 minutes, or until it reaches the soft-crack stage. Take off the heat, add the vanilla and walnuts, and stir it as it cools.

---

13) Cherry foam

2 cups gran sugar
½ cup water, without stirring
when syrup will thread add
¼ teasp vanilla pour slowly
on beaten whites of 2 eggs
beat until stiff & drop on
buttered paper. Before cool
press cherry on top.

In its original form, this recipe makes a very soft, unstable meringue that is impossible to pick up and eat as clearly intended—why else press a cherry into the top? Three things are wrong with this recipe: the temperature the sugar is cooked to is too low, the amount of sugar in proportion to the 2 egg whites is too high, and the product needs to be baked.

The recipe seems to be aiming for Italian meringue, where a hot sugar syrup (at softball stage) is beaten into whipped egg whites to make a stable, stiff meringue, but one that needs to be baked before it becomes something that can be picked up and eaten.

Mrs. Ayre tells us not to stir while the sugar is boiling, but this is to avoid crystallization of the sugar and applies only at higher temperatures than here; so stir if you wish.

It makes a neater finished product if the meringue is piped onto the baking sheets, but scooping out spoonfuls is fine, although never as tidy. This recipe makes about 16 pieces if each is about ¼ cup, more if made smaller.

CHERRY FOAM
makes 16 portions

½ cup (100 g) sugar
2 tablespoons (30 ml) water
2 egg whites
16 candied cherries (or more)

Preheat oven to 200°F. Boil the water and sugar to the soft-ball stage. While the sugar is boiling, whip the egg whites to soft peaks. When the sugar syrup is ready, give the whites a final whisk to stiff peaks, then pour the syrup in a thin stream onto the whipped egg whites, whipping continuously as you do so. When all the syrup is added, do not stop whipping—as you continue to whip, the mixture will stiffen further (but there is no need to whip until the mixture is cold, just until it has cooled slightly and stiffened as much as it is going to). Then scoop or pipe small portions (about ¼ cup) onto buttered paper, parchment paper, or a silicone mat. Press a candied cherry into the top of each. Bake for 1 hour. They will still be malleable and maybe a bit soft inside when straight from the oven, but will firm up as they cool. If you want them completely dry on the inside, bake another hour.

14) Plain fritter batter

is quickly made with 2 eggs beaten light (separate) to yolks add a tablesp butter melted 2 tablesp water flavouring, ½ cup sugar, sift 1 cup flour and add it & the stiff whites of eggs with as little beating as possible. The batter should be about as thick as thin cream sauce. Apricots peaches, or apples or any fruit may be halved or quartered and dipped in this batter & then fried quickly in boiling fat: Never pierce fritters with fork when lifting or will flatten Lift with slotted spoon. Drain a minute and sprinkle with powdered sugar. For apple fritters sugar may be seasoned with cinnamon & nutmeg.

This recipe needs modification because folding the flour and whipped whites into the very stiff yolk-sugar mixture is difficult, and the result is far thicker than the specified "thin cream sauce"—much too stiff for use as a frying batter. For a proper consistency, a total of about ¾ cup of water is needed.

How Mrs. Ayre judged the temperature of her boiling fat is not mentioned, but several methods were used at that time. One was to toss a small cube (½ inch) of white bread into the fat and see how long it took to go brown. At around the right temperature (360°F) bread cubes go golden brown in 15 to 30 seconds. Another method was to drop a sacrificial piece of whatever you were frying into the fat: if it bobbed to the surface more or less immediately, the fat was hot enough. These are interesting historical curiosities; use a thermometer in a saucepan of fat or a thermostatically controlled domestic deep fryer.

PLAIN FRITTER BATTER
makes about 2½ cups (625 ml) batter

2 egg yolks
1 tablespoon (15 g) melted butter
½ teaspoon (2.5 ml) vanilla

½ cup (100 g) sugar
¾ cup (190 ml) water
2 egg whites, whipped to soft peaks
1 cup (150 g) flour

Beat together the yolks, melted butter, vanilla, sugar, and water. Mix in the flour. Whip the whites to soft peaks and fold them into the yolk-flour mixture. If necessary, gently stir in 1 or 2 more tablespoons of water to get the batter as thin as whipping cream. Dip pieces of fruit in this batter and deep-fry in lard at around 360°F for about 4 to 6 minutes, until the batter is golden brown.

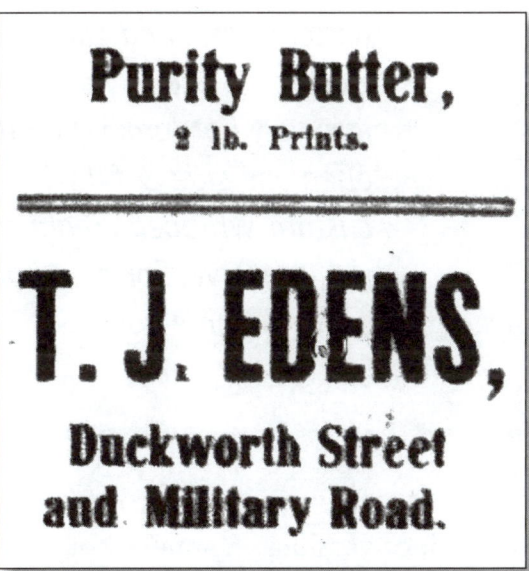

Evening Telegram, March 28, 1918.

15 Very rich fritters

are made as cream puffs are. Put ¼ cup butter 1 cup hot water 1 tablesp sugar & ¼ teasp salt into a granite pan. When this boils briskly turn in 1¼ cups sifted flour. Remove from the fire. Beat briskly with wire spoon and it will not lump but be smooth Add one at a time 4 unbeaten eggs and continue mixing until batter is cool and eggs well worked in. Drop by spoonfuls into very hot lard. When done open one side & fill with custard, whipped cream or rich preserve. Sprinkle powdered sugar & serve hot.

This is a cream-puff mixture (choux pastry), and the recipe approximates to modern versions. A small improvement is to keep the pan on a very low heat while beating in the flour (but before adding the eggs) to help dry out the dough. We made these with about 2 tablespoons of the dough (using a tablespoon measure with as much heaped above as in it). The dough gets very stiff and sticky, but if left to cool to room temperature portions can be formed into little spheres by rolling in your lightly greased palms. In the later stages of frying these fritters puff so much that they float mostly out of the fat, so turn them over occasionally with a slotted spoon.

VERY RICH FRITTERS
makes about 3½ cups (875 ml) batter

¼ cup (50 g) butter
1 cup (250 ml) water
1 tablespoon (12.5 g) sugar
¼ teaspoon (1.5 g) salt

1¼ cups (190 g) flour
4 eggs
whipped cream (or other filling)
icing sugar for dusting

Put the butter, water, sugar, and salt in a saucepan and bring to a boil. Dump in all the flour at once, reduce the heat to minimum, and stir vigorously until the dough is smooth and pulling away from the sides of the pan. Take the pan off the heat, and beat in the eggs one at a time, making sure each is incorporated before adding the next. Deep-fry spoonfuls of the dough in hot lard (360°F) for about 10 to 12 minutes, or until golden brown and plumped up to twice their original size. When cooked, drain on layers of paper towel. When cool enough to handle (and while the next batch is cooking), slit them open along one side and pipe in stiffly whipped cream (or very thick custard, stiff jam, or other preserve). Sprinkle with icing sugar and serve hot or warm.

16 Plain fritter batter

for meats &
vegetables is made with 2 beaten
eggs, 1 cups of flour ½ teasp salt
1 tablesp melted butter & enough
water to make thin batter. Many
cooks prefer this for croquettes
meatcakes etc. to breading

Do not try to beat in all the flour at once because it will make the batter so stiff that it is difficult to get the water in. Add no more than about half the flour to the beaten eggs before starting to alternate with portions of water. Use up all the flour with the ½ cup of water, but be prepared to add a few more tablespoons to thin the batter to the consistency of cream. This batter is not very inspiring but, as Mrs. Ayre suggests, can be used on pieces of meat or vegetables and on croquettes and meat cakes.

PLAIN FRITTER BATTER
makes about 2 cups (500 ml) batter

2 eggs
½ teaspoon (3.3 g) salt
1 tablespoon (15 g) melted butter

1 cup (150 g) flour
½ cup (125 ml) water

Beat the eggs, salt, and melted butter together. Then beat in the flour, alternating with portions of water. Mix in enough extra water to make a thin batter. Dip croquettes, meatballs, or pieces of vegetable in this and deep-fry in hot lard (360°F) for about 10 minutes, or until the batter is golden brown. Drain on paper towel and serve hot.

17. Orange Cream.

Make boiled custard but use cream instead of milk. Use only the yolks of the eggs in the custard & beat the whites very stiffly. Add them just before taking the custard from the boiler. Whites will rise to top. Add juice of 2 or 3 oranges and a little grated rind if you like it.

The basic recipe and method are the same as for recipe 55 for boiled custard. "Boiled" meant anything from a full rolling boil, through a gentle simmer, to something which gets nowhere near the boiling point, as in this custard. As with all custards, this will curdle if overheated. Coating a spoon is a traditional guide to when the custard has cooked enough, and with experience that is reliable. If you are unsure, use a thermometer and heat the mixture, stirring frequently, to no more than about 176°F.

Incorporating the whipped egg whites is problematic. If they are totally folded in, to make a completely homogeneous mixture, they deflate significantly and do not float to the surface afterwards as Mrs. Ayre says they will. But if they are not mixed in at all, they sit on top and slowly deflate and dissolve. She probably intended something between the two. This works if the whites are just folded in briefly, leaving them partly intact so that when they rise to the top they are coated in custard and flecks of orange zest but have not significantly deflated.

The orange juice thins this custard to a pouring consistency, which makes it difficult to serve. We found that you have to scoop up portions with a large spoon, making sure each portion gets some of the egg white floating on the top.

ORANGE CREAM
serves 6

2 cups (500 ml) cream
3 egg yolks
¼ cup (50 g) sugar
⅓ teaspoon (0.8 g) salt

3 egg whites, beaten stiff
juice of 2 or 3 oranges
grated orange zest

Beat the yolks with the sugar and salt and put in the top of a double boiler set over barely simmering water. Whisk in the cream and continue whisking until the mixture thickens and coats a spoon (or reaches 176°F). Whisk in the orange juice and zest. Whisk the egg whites to stiff peaks and briefly turn them over in the custard to more or less coat them. Turn this out into an 8 by 8-inch dish and leave to cool.

18. Toronto tea biscuit.

Cream ¼ cup
butter with ½ cup sugar add 1 beaten
egg 2 cups sifted flour containing
½ teasp salt & 2 teasps baking
powder. Flavour with ¼ cup orange
juice. Roll thin cut in rounds.
Spread each biscuit with butter
sugar & few nut meats cut small
bake in hot oven till lightly browned.

This basic biscuit formula makes a stiff dough which is difficult to get completely homogeneous, so turn it out of the mixing bowl and knead it on a lightly floured surface a few times until uniform. The instruction to "roll thin" is subjective, but rolling this amount of dough to about a 16-inch circle worked well.

The butter-sugar topping is presumably a standard mixture of a little butter with a lot of icing sugar, and just enough milk or water to achieve the desired consistency. The proportions given in the recipe below are based on accounts from the 1920s. The amount of milk or water can be adjusted by ½ teaspoon at a time to make a softer or firmer paste according to taste.

Mrs. Ayre's instructions are misleading, because it reads as though the biscuits are spread with topping before being baked, which seemed dubious. Nevertheless, we tried it: disaster. As expected, the butter-sugar topping melted and flowed off the biscuits. Despite her recipe, the topping goes on *after* the biscuits have been baked and have cooled.

For our taste, this is rather a dull biscuit, and not one we will be in a hurry to make again.

TORONTO TEA BISCUIT
makes 30 to 36 biscuits

¼ cup (50 g) butter
½ cup (100 g) sugar
1 egg
2 cups (300 g) flour

½ teaspoon (3.3 g) salt
2 teaspoons (10 g) baking powder
¼ cup (65 ml) orange juice

For the butter-sugar topping
1 tablespoon (15 g) butter
1 cup (120 g) icing sugar

5 teaspoons (25 ml) milk or water
½ cup (50 g) nuts

Preheat the oven to 350°F. Cream the butter and sugar together. Beat in the egg. Mix the flour, salt, and baking powder and beat into the butter mixture. Beat in the orange juice. Knead the dough a few times to ensure it is mixed well. Roll out on a lightly floured surface to about a 16-inch circle, which will be no more than about ⅛ inch thick. With a sharp-edged metal cutter, cut out 2½-inch circles. Re-roll the scraps and cut out more circles.

Bake on well-seasoned baking sheets (or baking parchment or silicone mats) for 15 to 17 minutes, or until the tops are lightly browned. Cool on racks.

For the topping, thoroughly mash together the icing sugar, butter, and water. Chop the nuts. Spread a small portion of this mixture (about ½ tsp) onto each biscuit, then press ½ teaspoon nuts into the mixture. Tip and shake off any nuts that have not stuck and re-use them.

---

19. Victoria Pudding.

Crumb enough stale lady fingers or sponge cake to fill pint cup. Mix with grated rind and juice of 3 oranges and 3 egg yolks. When smooth add ½ cup thin cream. Bake in dish or in pastry shells.

This is best made with stale sponge cake rather than lady fingers. The pint of sponge cake is about half an 8-inch cake. Made with either cake or lady fingers and baked in a pan, it makes a pleasant but soggy dessert. We prefer it in a pre-baked pastry shell, where the crisp pastry offsets and complements the moist filling. In both cases, it is improved by dollops of whipped cream.

VICTORIA PUDDING

makes one 8 by 8-inch (20 x 20 cm) pudding or one 9-inch (23 cm) tart

2 cups (150 g) stale crumbled sponge cake
juice and zest of 3 oranges
3 egg yolks
½ cup (125 ml) cream

Preheat the oven to 350°F. Break up the stale cake (or lady fingers) into crumbs by rubbing lightly between your fingers. Mix in the zest until any clumps are broken up. Beat the orange juice and egg yolks, and cream together until well mixed. Stir the juice mixture into the crumb-zest mixture until well combined. Pour into an 8 by 8-inch pan or a 9-inch pre-baked pastry shell. Bake about 30 minutes, or until the mixture has set. Serve warm.

20. Chicken + Chestnut Salad.

Cut up 3 cups cold cooked chicken into coarse pieces sprinkle over it a little salt & pepper. Boil in salted water until tender 3 doz chestnuts then chop into quarters. Slice 5 acid apples and mix all together moisten with a french dressing Serve on crisp lettuce leaves & garnish with pickled nasturtium seeds.

This and other salad recipes are not so much recipes as ideas. Much depends on the quality of the ingredients and the judicious hand of the cook. The chestnuts, for example, need to be this season's.

Tart apples are best in this salad, so don't use Mackintosh, which are all texture and little flavour, or Golden Delicious, which usually lack acidity unless very fresh. Granny Smith apples are ideal, but be wary as they are often old and tired, acidic without flavour, and often going rotten from within. In fact, any reasonably tart apple works well here, such as a Cortland.

What she meant by a French dressing is uncertain, but it was likely a vinaigrette as opposed to the sweet, thickened, commercial "French" dressings that were not available in her day. A good, basic vinaigrette can be made by vigorously shaking together

1 tablespoon of white wine vinegar, 3 tablespoons of olive oil, and 1 teaspoon of prepared French mustard.

Pickled nasturtium seeds were often used as a substitute for capers—but today pickled nasturtium seeds are in fact harder to find than capers, so use capers.

CHICKEN & CHESTNUT SALAD
serves 6 to 8

3 cups (700 g) cold, cooked chicken
salt and pepper to taste
36 chestnuts, whole, in their skins
5 tart apples

lettuce leaves
4 tablespoons (60 ml) vinaigrette
 or to taste
1 tablespoon (10 g) capers

Cut a shallow cross into the flat side of each chestnut. Just cover the chestnuts with water in a small pot and bring to a boil. Simmer for 5 or 10 minutes or until they can be easily pierced with the point of a small sharp knife poked through the cross. Drain. When just cool enough to handle, peel off the hard, brown outer skin and the thin, pale brown inner skin. Cut each peeled chestnut into about 4 pieces. Cut up the chicken into ½-inch cubes. Peel and core the apples, and cut them into pieces about the same size as the chicken pieces. Mix the chestnuts, chicken, and apples. Mix in about 4 tablespoons of vinaigrette, or more to taste. Arrange lettuce leaves on a serving dish and pile the chestnut-chicken salad on top. Rinse the capers (or nasturtium seeds) to eliminate excess pickle, drain well, and sprinkle over the salad.

21. Dutch Salad

Cut up 2 cups cold duck & a cup walnut meats in meat stock ~~simmer~~ for 5 minutes. Drain and cut into small pieces dice a large tart apple. Mix all together squeeze over it 2 teasp. each lemon & orange juice & moisten with mayonaise. Serve on cress leaves. Garnished with celery tips.

There is nothing particularly Dutch about duck, so was this a slip of the pen? Should it properly have been Duck Salad? We think so. Either way, this was clearly a way of making a meal out of leftovers. To get the requisite 2 cups of duck meat start with about half a large duck (at least 4 but preferably 5-pound dressed weight). Most likely you will be using leftover roast duck, but if you are cooking duck just for this salad, it can just as easily be poached in a large pot of water for 2 or 3 hours on a very low heat. Pick the lean meat off the bones, measure out what you need, and reserve any surplus for another use.

The instructions are confusing. She has clearly crossed out "simmer," but then the recipe makes no sense unless you do exactly that. So we simmered the cut-up duck and the nuts for 5 minutes. She used meat stock; we used commercial beef stock. Although Mrs. Ayre says to simmer the duck in chunks before cutting into smaller pieces, it is just as easy to cut the duck into small pieces before simmering. The same for the nuts: cut them into small dice before simmering. Walnuts were specified, but walnuts are too often tainted by rancidity, which will spoil this or any other salad. It's much safer to use pecans—the taste and texture are remarkably similar to walnuts, and they are much easier to find fresh and non-rancid.

Mix the simmered duck and nuts with the two juices before cutting up the apple, so that the apple dice can be mixed in quickly, before they go brown. We used a large

Cortland apple, but any large apple can be used.

Mrs. Ayre was familiar with mayonnaise (see recipe 7), and since no commercial mayonnaise was available in Newfoundland until the 1920s, she necessarily made her own. So in the interests of historical accuracy (but also because it tastes much better), make real mayonnaise for this recipe. But one shortcut is to use a good quality commercial product. This is one recipe that needs salt and pepper; she doesn't mention them, but we added both to our recipe.

She recommends cress as a background for this salad, but it is often hard to find, so substitute any lettuce of your choice if necessary. Use fresh, unwilted celery leaves for garnish—if you can't find them, omit the garnish or substitute parsley, the flat-leaved Italian variety.

DUCK SALAD
serves 4 to 6

2 cups (about 200 g) cooked duck meat
1 cup (100 g) walnuts or pecans
1 cup (250 ml) meat stock or beef broth
1 large (about 8 oz/225 g) apple
2 teaspoons (10 ml) orange juice
2 teaspoons (10 ml) lemon juice
¼ teaspoon (1.5 g) salt
¼ teaspoon (0.75 g) black pepper
3 tablespoons (45 ml) mayonnaise, or to taste
cress leaves (or lettuce of your choice)
small celery leaves for garnish

Cut the lean duck meat into small dice, about ½ inch or less. Cut the walnuts or pecans into small pieces, no bigger than the pieces of duck. Bring duck and nuts to a boil in the beef broth and simmer for 5 minutes. Drain and then toss with the orange juice, lemon juice, salt, and pepper. Peel and core the apple, then chop into pieces about the same size as the duck, and mix into the duck-nut mixture. Mix in mayonnaise to taste. Spread sprigs of cress (or lettuce) on a large platter, and carefully spoon the duck and nut salad on top, leaving plenty of green showing at the edges. Coarsely chop the celery leaves and sprinkle over the top.

22. Sardine Salad.

Remove bones from fish & serve on crisp lettuce leaves with strips of sweet red peppers scattered over it. Sprinkle with lemon juice & serve with french dressing garnished with stuffed olives.

Likely the sardines used in this recipe were larger ones, about 4 in a can, rather than the modern style where 16 or more small fish are crammed into one can. It is highly unlikely that she would specify removing the bones from the smaller fish—impossibly tedious—but entirely feasible with four to a can. We don't see the point of deboning any size of sardine, but since that's what she says, we followed suit.

We do know that she had a selection of sizes of cans of sardines available to her. For example, The Royal Stores of St. John's advertised in the *Evening Telegram* in 1902 that they had sardines in 7-, 12-, and 17-cent tins, but how big the fish were and how many in a can is unknown. She also had a choice between sardines in oil and sardines in tomato. As there is no way of knowing which she used, and since oil-packed sardines were the mainstream, we used those in this recipe.

The red pepper is problematic. She may have been referring to a fresh red pepper, but there is no evidence these were available in St. John's at that time (although fresh green peppers were sometimes advertised). She may have meant pickled, bottled red pepper, sometimes sold as red pimento, which is what we used here. And as in the chicken and chestnut salad (recipe 20), we assume by French dressing she meant a vinaigrette (see recipe 20 for making basic vinaigrette).

Any crisp lettuce works well here, such as romaine or Boston. The stuffed olives are often sold as Manzanilla olives with pimento.

SARDINE SALAD
serves 4

- 8 large (each about 1 oz/25 g) canned sardines
- 4-ounce (112 g) jar pickled red pepper
- 1 tablespoon (15 ml) lemon juice
- lettuce leaves of your choice
- 2 tablespoons (30 ml) vinaigrette
- 12 green olives stuffed with pimento

Drain the sardines. Lay each on its side, and carefully cut down the back with a small, sharp knife. Lift the top fillet from the fish. Carefully pick the backbone and any attached ribs from the lower fillet. Reserve the deboned fillets. Spread lettuce leaves over a large platter and arrange the sardine fillets on top. Cut the red pepper into very thin slivers and place these on top of the sardines and lettuce. Sprinkle everything with lemon juice, and then drizzle the vinaigrette over the lot. Garnish with stuffed olives.

---

23. Corn Cakes.

Press ½ can corn
through a sieve to remove all the pulp
Add 1 cup rich milk 2 beaten eggs
1 teasp sugar and ½ teasp salt &
1½ cups flour containing 2 teasp baking
powder. Bake in pudding dish or in
gem pans.

How much was half a can of corn? Cans in Mrs. Ayre's day were usually 1 pound or ½ pound, and not much else, except for flat sardine cans and much bigger ones holding several pounds. Today most canned corn seems to be 340 millilitres net volume and are 1-pound cans—the empty can holds almost exactly 450 millilitres (1 lb) of water when filled to the brim. So a 1-pound can contains about 12 ounces (340 g) drained weight corn. If her half can is ½ pound, that translates into 6 ounces (170 g) of drained weight corn. That amount of corn makes a cake that is not very corny—in fact twice that amount (i.e., a 1 lb can, 340 g drained weight corn) makes a better cake.

Be warned about her simple instruction to press the corn through a sieve. First, don't try to push it through with a flexible rubber spatula. Tough corn kernels need the edge of a wide wooden spoon to crush and squeeze them. Breaking up the corn first in a food processor helps, but not as much as we hoped—it took another 10 or more minutes of hard rubbing to get the corn through the sieve.

As so often, she does not specify size of pan, baking temperature, or time. The instructions given here are the results of experimentation. The gem pans she mentions both here and elsewhere were commonplace. They were essentially muffin pans, typically 6 or 12 receptacles to a unit. They were cast iron, often with spaces between the receptacles to let the oven heat circulate. The shape and size of the receptacles varied, from a typical muffin shape, through shallow pans like mini cake pans, to corn-cob shapes for small cornbreads. We baked the cake in a small loaf pan.

This recipe makes rather neutral-tasting cakes, much improved by the addition of butter and jam, so maybe these were intended as snack food or for afternoon tea. They are also good slathered with butter and eaten with baked beans.

CORN CAKES
makes one 4 by 8-inch (10 x 20 cm) loaf

half of one 340-millilitre can, drained weight (170 g) canned corn
2 eggs
1 teaspoon (4 g) sugar
½ teaspoon (3.3 g) salt
2 teaspoons (10 g) baking powder
1 cup (250 ml) milk
1½ cups (225 g) flour

Preheat the oven to 350°F. Grease and flour a small loaf pan, about 4½ by 8½ inches. Drain the corn, then mash through a sieve. Beat the eggs and mix with the corn. Mix in the sugar, salt, and baking powder. Add portions of flour and milk alternately, keeping the dough fairly stiff to avoid lumps until all the flour is added, then add the rest of the milk. Press the dough evenly into the prepared pan. Bake for 50 to 60 minutes, or until a small skewer inserted in the thickest part comes out clean. Turn out on a rack.

24. Apple + Tapioca pudding.

Soak the tapioca or prepare it as directed Cook it until transparent & pour it into a pudding dish. Add beaten yolks of 2 eggs & cup milk to each cup tapioca. Flavour & add pint thick sweet apple sauce. Grate nutmeg over top & put in oven. Beat whites of eggs stiff and sweeten Them. Season with cinnamon Heap this on pudding & brown nicely. Serve very cold.

Tapioca comes either as small spheres, which need soaking overnight, or in a granular form (like coarsely granulated sugar), which needs only a brief soaking. The recipe's instructions seem to cover both. Tapioca cooks to a gelatinous, translucent mass, and if the small-sphere form was used, the result bears an uncanny resemblance to frog-spawn, which is exactly what English schoolboys called it.

And that cup of tapioca in her recipe, is it before or after soaking and cooking? Surely she means after, because a full cup of uncooked would generate 2 quarts of cooked, gelatinous tapioca—disproportionate to the rest of the recipe. It seems clear that the yolks, milk, flavouring, and applesauce are to be simply mixed with the cooked tapioca. Her instructions to put it in the oven before beating the egg whites seems pointless because there are not enough egg yolks to set the mass, even with the aid of the gelatinous tapioca. So does the egg-white topping go on before the whole thing goes in the oven?

Both ways were tested, and it seems to work best if the tapioca mixture is not baked before the topping, which means that if you are suspicious of uncooked (or undercooked) egg yolks, avoid this recipe. It works best in a pudding basin, with the egg-white topping spread thickly on top. Mrs. Ayre does not specify how much to sweeten the egg whites; but as sugar stabilizes the whipped whites, use between ¼ and ½ cup of sugar for 2 egg whites. After much trial and error (mostly error), here is a version that works, more or less.

APPLE & TAPIOCA PUDDING
serves 4 to 6

2 tablespoons (24 g) granulated tapioca
1 cup (250 ml) water
2 egg yolks
1 cup (250 ml) milk

2 cups (500 ml) thick applesauce (recipe below)
½ teaspoon (2.5 ml) vanilla
¼ teaspoon (0.75 g) nutmeg

Topping
2 egg whites
¼–½ cup (50–100 g) sugar

pinch cinnamon

Applesauce
4 medium (about 28 oz/800 g, untrimmed total; 14 oz/400 g, trimmed total) apples
½ cup (125 ml) water
½ cup (100 g) sugar

Preheat the oven to 400°F. Peel and core the apples and slice thinly. Bring them to a boil in the water with the sugar. Simmer until the apples have broken down into mush. If they do not break down easily, mash with a potato masher when they are completely soft. Makes about 2 cups of thick sauce.

Soak the tapioca in the water for about 10 minutes. Bring to a boil and simmer gently for about 5 minutes, or until the mixture goes translucent. Take off the heat and let cool.

Grease a 2-quart pudding basin. Thoroughly mix the egg yolks, milk, and vanilla with the cooked tapioca. Pour and scrape into the prepared basin, and sprinkle the grated nutmeg on top. Whip the egg whites to soft peaks, then whip in the sugar until stiff peaks have formed. Spread the whipped whites on top of the tapioca mixture. Bake for about 15 minutes until the whites are browned on top. Cool, and then refrigerate.

25. Baked Omelette.

Beat yolks
& whites of 4 eggs separately
when very light add 4 tablesp
sifted flour to the yolks, 1 tablesp
melted butter, 4 tablesp milk
1 teasp salt 1 sugar. Last
moment add whites. Put into a
buttered baking dish and bake
20 minutes in hot oven. Must be
covered first 15 minutes.

There are three problems with this recipe. First, the yolk-flour mixture is too fluid and impossible to fold into the whipped whites; it sinks and makes a dense layer on the bottom of the omelette. Stirring them together deflates the egg whites, which defeats the point of whipping them separately. Second, it is too salty. Third, the sugar is too evident. The recipe below is adjusted to address these points. In addition, but not as important, there is no need to cover it for the first 15 minutes. Covering stops it from browning; not covering results in a nicely golden top.

Mrs. Ayre gives no indication what size baking dish to use; the one mentioned below works well.

BAKED OMELETTE
serves 2 to 4

4 eggs
½ cup (75 g) flour
1 tablespoon (15 g) melted butter

½ teaspoon (3.3 g) salt
½ teaspoon (2 g) sugar
4 tablespoons (60 ml) milk

Preheat the oven to 400°F. Grease an 8 by 8-inch baking pan. Separate the yolks and whites of the eggs. Mix the salt, sugar, and milk with the yolks until completely combined. Mix in the flour until very smooth. Beat the egg whites to stiff peaks. Fold the yolk mixture into the beaten whites until well combined. Pour and scrape this into the prepared pan. Bake for about 20 minutes, or until the top has browned. For a less brown top, cover the pan with a square of foil for the first 10 or 15 minutes. Serve immediately.

26. Washington Pie.

Beat 3 eggs separately & to the yolks add 1 cup sugar 2 cups flour. 3 teasps baking powder & a teasp vanilla. Fold in whites bake in jelly cake tins 8 minutes.

Washington Pie is from America, where it was also called Martha Washington Pie, or Washington Cake, and printed recipes date from 1878. It is not a pie with pastry, but a layer cake, with jam or preserve between the layers and a decorative dusting of fine sugar on top. The American versions often have three or four layers of cake with a variety of jams or marmalades between them. Newfoundland versions usually had only two layers, often with blueberry, partridgeberry, or bakeapple jams in the middle.

The basic formula is problematic because the recipe does not mention any fluid in the batter. Just in case, we tried it exactly as she describes it. The yolks, sugar, and flour make a dry, coarsely granular mixture, which make an unholy mess when folded with the egg whites. No, she missed the fluid; the recipe below puts it back.

Although "Washington Pie" means that this is a layer cake, the recipe does not indicate how many layers. After experimenting, it seems clear she was aiming for two shallow cakes—that amount of batter spread over three or more cakes does not work.

WASHINGTON PIE
makes one 8-inch (20 cm), 2-layer cake

3 eggs, separated
1 cup (200 g) sugar
2 cups (300 g) flour
1 teaspoon (5 ml) vanilla
3 teaspoons (15 g) baking powder
1¼ cups (310 ml) milk

To finish
1 cup (250 ml) jam of your choice 1 tablespoon (7.5 g) icing sugar to dust

Preheat the oven to 350°F. Grease and flour two 8-inch cake pans. Mix the yolks with the sugar, flour, vanilla, and baking powder. Beat in the milk. Beat the whites to stiff peaks and fold into the batter. Divide mixture between the prepared cake pans and bake for about 20 minutes, or until a small skewer inserted into the thickest part comes out clean. Turn out onto racks to cool. When cool, reserve the tidiest looking cake for the top. Skim a layer off the top of the other one to make a flat surface and spread the jam on it. Carefully lower the reserved cake onto the jam. Put the icing sugar in a fine-mesh sieve and tap the edge to dust the top of the cake.

28. Kriss Kringle Whip.

*Core and pare
3 apples. Remove stones from dates
Put ½ cup dates ½ cup nuts through
food chopper. Grate apples. Beat
2 egg whites with beater until
stiff & fluffy. Fold stiffly beaten
egg whites into the combined fruit
& nuts. Serve in stemmed glasses
with whipped cream and cherries.*

A food chopper is usually known as a food grinder (US term) or food mincer (UK term) today. Chopping dates or nuts in a food grinder has never worked for us. It compresses the dates and extrudes long, sticky, brown ropes, and squeezes the oil out of nuts—even using the plate with the largest holes (⅜ inch). Food grinders were no different in Mrs. Ayre's day; early 19th-century models were much the same as today's, apart from being better made. So the dates and nuts need to be chopped by hand. The dates can be problematic because they are so sticky; so after a few initial cuts, sprinkle with sugar and continue chopping. We suggest using pecans rather than walnuts: the two are interchangeable in any recipe, and walnuts are often tainted by rancidity.

If the egg whites are whipped without sugar, as the recipe suggests, they will start to break down and ooze fluid after only 5 minutes—very unpleasant. Whipping with some sugar, about 2 tablespoons per egg white, stabilizes the whites so that they will not break down for many hours.

Make sure the egg whites are whipped before grating the apples. To prevent them from going brown, grate them directly into the whipped whites.

KRISS KRINGLE WHIP
serves 6

3 apples
½ cup (75 g) chopped dates
1 tablespoon (12.5 g) sugar, plus extra for chopping the dates
½ cup (50 g) walnuts
2 egg whites
¼ cup (50 g) sugar
½ cup (125 ml) cream, or more to taste
6 candied cherries

If there are pits in the dates, slit them lengthways and remove the pits. Cut dates into ¼-inch pieces, sprinkling with a little sugar to prevent them from clumping together and sticking to your knife. Chop walnuts until no piece is bigger than about ¼ inch. Whip the egg whites to soft peaks, then add the sugar in portions while continuing to whip to glossy stiff peaks. Peel and core the apples, and grate directly into the whipped egg whites, mixing as you go to prevent the apples from browning. Fold in the chopped dates and nuts. Divide between 6 stemmed glasses. Whip the cream, divide between the glasses, and smooth the tops with the back of a small spoon. Top each with a candied cherry.

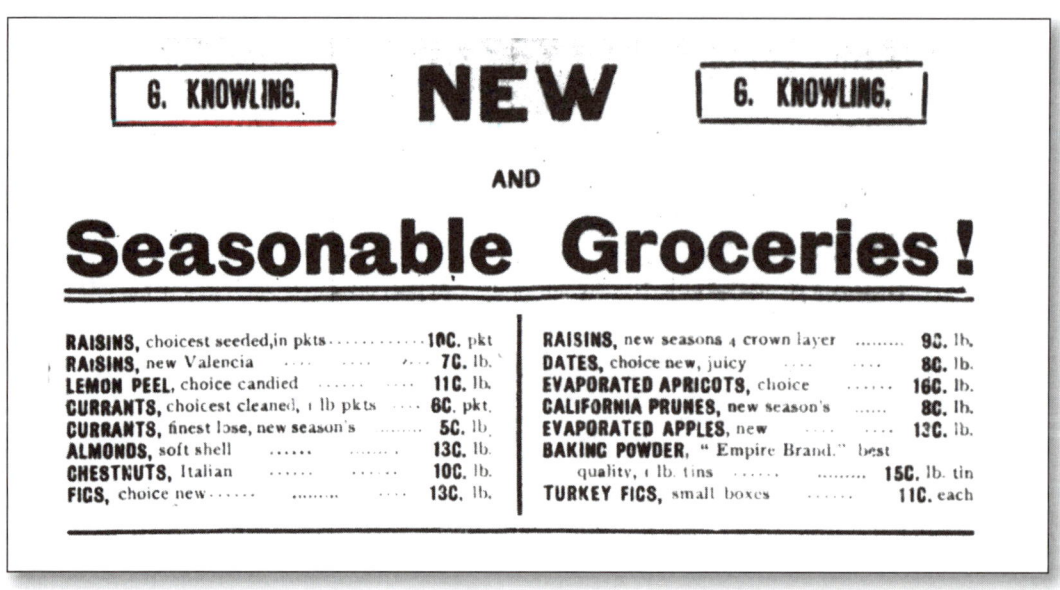

Evening Telegram, December 22, 1909.

29. Dandelions.

Serve boiled with cream sauce. Or like spinach with poached eggs. For soup use 1 cup chopped fine 3 cups nice stock 1 cup milk 2 tablesps butter 2 tablesps flour 1 teasp grated onion salt pepper. Mash through wire strainer add to stock. Melt butter add flour stir till smooth. Add to soup & boil for 5 minutes. For salad cut leaves very fine sharp knife same as celery & serve with dressing. Another way is to mix with cream or cottage cheese & fill tomato.

Dandelion leaves were traditionally relished as one of the first greens in the spring, a refreshing change from the root vegetables of winter. The trick with dandelion leaves, no matter what they are used for, is to pick them young and fresh, when their natural bitterness is at a minimum. As Mrs. Ayre herself said, "Early in May crowds of Dandelion-pickers fill their baskets with 'greens,' more delicious to a Newfoundland palate than any other. They must be gathered before the flowers come, as then they are bitter."

As with any loose leaves, it is difficult to work in cups, but here 1 cup of loosely packed dandelion leaves equals about $2/3$ ounces.

Traditionally, dandelion leaves were well boiled, but we prefer shorter cooking times. Depending on the age of the leaves, between 5 and 10 minutes is usually about right. Although 16 cups of leaves may look like a lot, they reduce significantly when boiled. The cream sauce is a béchamel.

BOILED DANDELION LEAVES
serves 4

16 cups (about 320 g) dandelion leaves   **½ cup (125 ml) béchamel sauce**

Make the béchamel ahead of time and keep warm or reheat when needed. Trim any damage from the dandelion leaves and cut off the stalk ends. Wash the leaves well. Bring a pot of lightly salted water to a boil and add the trimmed dandelion leaves. Boil the leaves about 10 minutes, then check for tenderness. Cook longer as desired. Drain the cooked leaves well, pressing on them lightly to remove the surplus water. Then mix thoroughly with the warm béchamel and serve immediately as a side vegetable.

The other cooked dandelion-leaf suggestion is to use them like spinach under poached eggs, but she gives no particular instructions.

DANDELION & POACHED EGGS
serves 4

8 cups (about 160 g) dandelion leaves   **butter for the bread**
4 thick slices bread   **8 eggs**

Trim any damage from the dandelion leaves and cut off the stalk ends. Wash the leaves well. Bring a pot of lightly salted water to a boil and add the trimmed dandelion leaves. Boil the leaves about 10 minutes, then check for tenderness. Cook longer as desired. Drain the cooked leaves well, pressing on them lightly to remove the surplus water. Reserve and keep warm. Poach the eggs to taste. Toast and butter the bread. Divide the cooked dandelion between the slices of buttered toast and roughly spread them out to cover the toast. Place 2 poached eggs on top of each slice of toast and dandelions, and serve at once.

Mrs. Ayre's dandelion soup recipe is confusing because the instructions are to add the strained vegetables to the stock when, in fact, they have already been cooked in the stock; nor does she say when to add the milk. We have revised her method to make it workable.

For the grated onion, chop a small amount of onion finely and take 1 teaspoon of that—or use a whole small onion, it can only improve this soup. Pushing the cooked dandelions through a strainer takes work, so use the edge of a wide wooden spoon to do so. A great deal of the mashed dandelion leaves gets stuck in the strainer, making cleanup difficult. It is more convenient, if less historically correct, to simply blend the mixture. This makes a light and pleasant soup, but it is really only as good as the stock used, so do not make this with water or a stock cube.

DANDELION SOUP
serves 4

1 cup (20 g) dandelion leaves
1 teaspoon (5 ml) grated onion
3 cups (750 ml) chicken stock
1 cup (250 ml) milk

2 tablespoons (30 g) butter
2 tablespoons (20 g) flour
½ teaspoon (3.3 g) salt
¼ teaspoon (1.5 g) pepper

Chop the dandelion leaves. Put them in the stock with the grated onion, bring to a boil and simmer about 15 minutes. Pour the liquid through a sieve and mash the solids through the mesh with the edge of a wide wooden spoon (or blend). Meanwhile, melt the butter in another pan, stir in the flour, and cook for 3 or 4 minutes, then add the milk and bring back to a boil, stirring as it thickens. Add salt and pepper. Pour the mashed dandelion and stock mixture into the thickened milk, stir together well, return to a boil, and simmer another 10 minutes. Taste and adjust the seasoning.

Last are two recipes in which the dandelion leaves are used raw, so here it is particularly important to use small, young leaves, because any excessive bitterness will be obvious. For the basic salad, a vinaigrette works well if the leaves are young and delicate. But in general, homemade mayonnaise is probably the best because its creaminess complements and softens the bitter edge of the leaves. The amount of dressing is a matter of taste.

DANDELION SALAD
serves 4

6 cups (about 120 g) dandelion leaves
2 tablespoons (30 ml) vinaigrette
   or mayonnaise

salt and pepper to taste

Trim any damage from the dandelion leaves and cut off the stalk ends. Wash the leaves well. Dry on a cloth (or in a salad spinner). Stack some of the leaves on a cutting board and sliver very thinly; repeat with the rest of the leaves. Toss the slivered leaves with vinaigrette or mayonnaise according to taste.

The raw leaves can be used to stuff tomatoes, and this is a good way of using up a few leaves if they are in short supply. The large tomatoes we used were about 6 ounces each and 3 inches in diameter.

TOMATOES WITH DANDELION & COTTAGE CHEESE
serves 4

4 large tomatoes (or more smaller ones)
2 cups (40 g) dandelion leaves

1 cup (250 g) cottage cheese

Cut the top off the tomatoes about one-third of the way down from the stem end. Discard the cut-off portions. Cut a thin sliver off the other end so that the tomato will stand level on a plate. Scoop out the flesh and seeds from the tomatoes with a small spoon or melon baller. Place them cut-side down on paper towel to drain completely while you make the filling. Trim any damage from the dandelion leaves and cut off the stalk ends. Wash the leaves well. Dry on a cloth (or in a salad spinner). Stack the leaves on a cutting board and sliver very thinly, then mix with the cottage cheese. Divide this mixture between the empty tomato shells.

30) Beef barley stew.

1 lb lean
stewing meat 2 cups canned tomatoes
2 teasp salt 4 tablesps flour
2 cups pearl barley ½ cup cut
celery or 2 tablesp dried celery
tops. Cut meat small, put on
in 4 cups of boiling water, boil
30 minutes then add well washed
barley boil slowly 1½ hours
add tomatoes, either strained
or mashed seasoning and flour
which has been mixed smooth
in a little cold water. A cup
cut carrot is an addition.

The amount of barley in this recipe is astonishing, but on the principle of following her recipe exactly for the first attempt, we tried the full 2 cups. First impressions were correct: the stew seized up solid in 20 minutes, leaving no fluid to thicken with flour. To have some fluid left to be thickened by the flour, no more than ⅓ cup of barley is needed. Mrs. Ayre recommends washing the barley before using it, perhaps to remove debris and insects; this is not necessary.

There is no need to boil the water the beef is going into—just bring the beef and water to a boil and then simmer. Add the salt with the second stewing, because if it is all added at the end it will not have time to permeate the chunks in the stew. If the salt is added at the end, it is best to leave the stew overnight and reheat the next day. Rather than straining or mashing the canned tomatoes, it is easier to chop them in small pieces.

Adding the carrot helps to improve the flavour, but overall it is a bland stew.

BEEF BARLEY STEW

serves 4 to 6

1 pound (450 g) lean stewing beef
4 cups (1 l) water
⅓ cup (60 g) barley
½ cup (50 g) celery
1 cup (150 g) chopped carrot
2 cups (500 ml) canned tomatoes
2 teaspoons (13 g) salt
2 tablespoons (20 g) flour

Trim the beef and cut into ½ to ¾-inch cubes. Put the beef and water in a large saucepan and bring to a boil. Simmer about 30 minutes. Trim the celery and chop into ¼-inch slices. Trim and chop the carrot into ½ to ¾-inch cubes. Add the barley, celery, carrot, and salt to the beef and water. Return to a boil and then simmer about 90 minutes. Chop the tomatoes and add to the stew. Bring back to a simmer. Mash the flour with a little water, taking care to avoid making lumps, then add it to the stew and simmer for another 10 minutes.

31. Baked macaroni + meat flavour

2 cups macaroni
2 cups tomatoes
½ cup meat scraps & gravy or bacon cut fine
½ cup cut onion ¼ teasp paprik
1 cup grated cheese ⅛ pepper
1 tablesp butter 2 teasp salt
Break macaroni into 1 inch or 2 inch pieces put into saucepan with 3 qts boiling water boil for 30 minutes then blanch with cold water. Butter baking dish put in macaroni & pour over it following sauce:
Sauce - Put bacon into frying pan add onion and fry until a light yellow not brown & hard, add 2 cup tomatoes salt pepper & paprika and ½ cup hot water, boil for 5 mins add cheese & pour over macaroni Put in hot oven and bake 20 – 25 mins or until light brown.

Macaroni was one of the first pastas to be imported into Newfoundland. Advertisements for it appeared in the St. John's *Evening Telegram* from the 1880s onwards, where it was often called "Naples Macaroni." In those days macaroni came as long tubes, which you broke into short lengths, although advertisements for "cut macaroni" appeared around the time Mrs. Ayre was penning her recipes. Long tubes of uncut macaroni are difficult to find now; mostly it is pre-cut and in the shape of little elbows. If you want to imitate her short, straight lengths of tube, use something like pennette (diminutive form of penne), which are short tubes slightly over 1 inch long, just like the lengths in the recipe. Cooking the macaroni for 30 minutes may offend modern sensibilities, but they liked things well cooked back then.

The 2 cups of tomatoes were presumably canned. The recipe does not work if the tomatoes are left whole or in large chunks, so chop before using them. The paprika is an oddity—there is so little of it that it can be omitted without altering either taste or appearance.

BAKED MACARONI & MEAT FLAVOUR
serves 6

- 2 cups (250 g) short lengths or elbows of macaroni
- ½ cup (70 g) bacon cubes
- ½ cup (70 g) onion (1 small onion)
- ¼ teaspoon (0.75 g) paprika
- 2 teaspoons (13 g) salt
- ⅛ teaspoon (0.4 g) ground pepper
- ½ cup (125 ml) hot water
- 1 cup (75 g) grated cheese
- 2 cups (500 ml) canned tomatoes
- 1 tablespoon (15 g) butter to grease dish

In a large pot, bring 3 quarts of water to a boil. Do not add salt. Add the macaroni, bring back to a boil, and cook for 30 minutes. While it is cooking, make the tomato sauce.

Drain the juice from the tomatoes and reserve. Chop the tomatoes, then mix them back with the juice. Chop the bacon into about ¼-inch pieces. Chop the onion the same size. Mix the bacon and onion and fry on a low heat until the onion is translucent and the bacon has rendered a little of its fat but has not become crisp. Add the reserved tomato, salt, pepper, paprika, and hot water. Bring to a boil and simmer for 5 minutes. Just before pouring it over the pasta, add the grated cheese and mix well. Have the tomato sauce ready before the pasta is cooked—the pasta will stick together if it stands too long.

Preheat the oven to 350°F, drain in a colander, and stand the colander of cooked pasta in a sink full of cold water. Drain the cold macaroni well, stirring it around in the colander to make sure that all the surplus water drains from the pasta tubes. Grease a baking dish (9 x 12 inches) with the butter. Spread the cooked macaroni in the baking dish, immediately pour the tomato sauce over the macaroni, and stir it to mix well. Bake for about 30 minutes, or until the top is flecked with brown.

32) Macaroni Croquettes

*2 cups macaroni 3 tablesps ch. boiled bacon
1 cup milk, 2 tablesps butter –
4 tablesp flour   1 cup grated cheese
1 teasp onion juice   1 teasp chopped
parsley or celery top, 1 teasp salt
a dash white pepper dash paprika
1 teasp w. sauce 1 egg. Bread crumbs.
Boil macaroni, put through food
chopper, add cream sauce bacon
& parsley. Mix well spread on
platter & set aside to cool. When
stiff and cold take a large spoon ful
into floured hands form into
cone shapes, dip in egg (one egg
beaten with 1 tablesp cold milk)
then in bread crumbs. Fry in deep
hot fat. Serve on platter with
tomato sauce. Garnish with sprigs
of parsley. This amount will make
six large croquettes.
Cream sauce. Melt butter add
flour   -   then milk slowly. When
thick grated cheese onion salt
pepper, paprika & sauce. Boil 1 minute*

See recipe 31 for comments on macaroni. We think it better to chop the cooked macaroni by hand to give a slightly coarser texture. But if you prefer to follow Mrs. Ayre's method for historical accuracy, put the macaroni through a food chopper (food grinder), particularly if you like a finer texture in the finished croquette.

A joint of boiled bacon would have been commonplace in the middle-class kitchens of Mrs. Ayre's day, although it is a rarity now. Substitute small cubes of any kind of bacon, between ⅛ and ¼ inch, poached briefly in water to cook through. Chopped celery leaves ("celery tops") occur here and elsewhere, and their mild but distinct flavour is an improvement over parsley.

The white sauce is a fairly standard béchamel, although today the rule of thumb is equal parts butter and flour—Mrs. Ayre was being frugal in using half the butter we would. The "w." sauce was undoubtedly Worcestershire sauce, available in Newfoundland at least as early as the 1880s, when (as now) Lea and Perrins was the principal brand to which others were compared.

Onion juice was made on the spot: cut a small onion in half and scrape at the exposed surface with the edge of a small, sharp knife. If this is too tedious, use the same amount of very finely chopped onion. The only reason to use juice rather than chopped onion is when you don't want the texture of chopped onion, but this does not apply here—there is so much other texture.

The recipe specifies forming the finished mixture into cones. This shape seems of doubtful value, and we found it best to shape into the more traditional cylindrical croquettes. The bread crumbs can be dry or fresh—the latter made by rubbing slices of stale bread between the fingers. Dry bread crumbs work better. If you use fresh, you will need slightly more than dry. We do not know what fat was used for frying, but both lard and shortening were available. We used lard. For more information on deep-frying, see recipe 14.

If you want to serve with a tomato sauce authentic to the period, use the sauce in recipe 31 but omit the cheese. These make a surprisingly pleasant starchy accompaniment to a variety of dishes.

MACARONI CROQUETTES
serves 6

2 cups (250 g) dry macaroni

For the sauce

2 tablespoons (30 g) butter
4 tablespoons (40 g) flour
1 cup (250 ml) milk
1 teaspoon (5 ml) onion juice
1 teaspoon (1.5 g) chopped celery leaf
1 teaspoon (6.5 g) salt
dash (0.25 g) white pepper
dash (0.25 g) paprika
1 teaspoon (5 ml) Worcestershire sauce
1 cup (75 g) grated cheese
3 tablespoons (25 g) chopped boiled bacon

For frying

1 egg
1 tablespoon (15 ml) milk
¾ cup (60 g) dry bread crumbs or 1 cup (80 g) from stale bread
lard for deep-frying

Bring 3 quarts of water to a boil in a large pot (5–6 qt). Do not add salt. Add the macaroni, return to a boil, and cook for 30 minutes.

Meanwhile, make the cream sauce. If you are using regular bacon, cut it into small cubes and poach in simmering water for 2 or 3 minutes. Then drain and reserve. Melt the butter in a small saucepan, stir in the flour until well mixed, add the milk, and bring to a simmer, stirring frequently. Stir in the onion juice, chopped celery leaf (or parsley), salt, white pepper, paprika, Worcestershire sauce, grated cheese, and poached bacon cubes. Reserve the sauce.

When the macaroni has cooked for 30 minutes, drain in a colander. Then either put the cooked macaroni through a food grinder or chop by hand. Thoroughly mix the ground or chopped pasta with the reserved sauce, and spread the mixture out on a flat pan (a 9 by 12-inch baking pan is a useful size) and leave to cool. When cool, divide into 6 equal portions. With floured hands, and on a lightly floured surface, press each portion tightly together and form into a cylinder, about three times longer than wide.

Heat the lard to deep-frying temperature (360°F). Beat the egg with 1 tablespoon of milk. Have the beaten egg and bread crumbs ready in shallow pans. Roll each croquette in the egg, shake off the surplus, and then roll in the bread crumbs. Drop as many breaded croquettes in the hot fat as will comfortably fit. Fry about 10 minutes, or until richly browned on the outside and hot on the inside. Drain and reserve on paper towels. Fry the remaining croquettes. Serve with warm tomato sauce.

33. Chocolate Sponge Roll.

1 ¼ cup flour
½ teasp salt
1 cup sugar
2 eggs
2 sqs melted chocolate
2 tablesp melted shortening
¼ cup hot water
1 teasp vanilla
2 teasps royal baking powder

Beat whole eggs. Add slowly sugar and boiling water add vanilla melted chocolate & melted shortening without beating. Add dry ingredients which have been sifted together three times and fold in as lightly as possible. Pour into large baking pan lined with oiled paper. ½ inch batter should not be more bake in slow oven 20 minute. When done turn on damp hot cloth spread with white icing roll & ice if liked.

Mrs. Ayre got this recipe from an advertisement for Royal baking powder in the *Evening Telegram*. As mentioned in the Introduction, manufacturers sometimes put recipes in their advertisements to encourage use of their product.

Then as now, chocolate often came in handy 1-ounce squares. Mrs. Ayre does not specify her method of melting chocolate, but likely it was in a basin set over simmering water—still one of the best ways. At least two brands of commercial shortening (solidified vegetable oils) were available: Crisco and Snowdrift. We used Crisco, although there is no guarantee that it is the same thing it was in her day.

Sifting eliminated clumps in flour and also served to mix dry ingredients. By all means sift the ingredients together here, but a thorough mixing in a bowl will suffice. The size of baking pan is not specified, but the batter should be no more than ½ inch in depth. A 9 by 12-inch pan works well—the batter will be about ⅜ inch thick.

Lining the pan with oiled paper would have created a non-stick surface. To be historically correct, take a rectangle of brown paper, brush it lightly with vegetable oil, and press it into the pan. More conveniently, use parchment paper.

Turning the cake out onto a damp tea towel is a good idea because even though the top of the baked cake (i.e., the surface which will go down on the towel) will have a thin crust, the dampness stops it from sticking. When the cake is lying on the towel, it can be spread with icing, and we think it is better for at least a skim of icing of some sort. Use any icing—you will need about 1 cup to spread thinly over the cake surface. If the icing is soft, be careful not to spread it close to the edge, because when it is rolled or folded, it will ooze out. Then after rolling or folding the cake, dust the top with icing sugar.

This cake is difficult to roll because it cracks easily. After repeated failed rolls, we wondered if Mrs. Ayre had actually ever made this cake. It is much more manageable to fold the cake like a letter, into three layers. To do this, lightly score the cake in two places to mark off three equal parts, then flip the thirds one over the other(s) to make a triple-layered cake.

CHOCOLATE SPONGE ROLL
makes one 9-inch (23 cm) roll

- 2 tablespoons (30 g) shortening
- 2 squares (60 g) semi-sweet baking chocolate
- 2 eggs
- 1 cup (200 g) sugar
- ¼ cup (60 ml) hot water
- 1 teaspoon (5 ml) vanilla
- 1¼ cups (190 g) flour
- ½ teaspoon (3.3 g) salt
- 2 teaspoons (10 g) baking powder

Preheat the oven to 325°F. Line a 9 by 12-inch rimmed pan with parchment paper. Put the chocolate and shortening in a bowl over barely simmering hot water and let melt. When melted, mix well and reserve. Beat the eggs until pale and fluffy, then add the sugar in small portions, beating continuously. Beat in the vanilla and hot water. Then gently mix in the melted chocolate and shortening. Thoroughly mix the flour, salt, and baking powder. Fold this mixture into the egg-chocolate mixture until no stray pockets of flour are left. Pour and scrape this into the lined baking pan. Bake for about 25 to 30 minutes.

Soak a tea towel in warm water and wring it as dry as possible. Spread the towel on the counter and turn the flat cake out onto it. Very carefully peel off the oiled or parchment paper; whenever the cake looks like it is sticking, gently scrape it free with a small knife or spatula and continue peeling off the paper. At this point the surface of the cake can be spread with icing or not, and then rolled into a fat cylinder or folded into a three-layered cake. Either way, dust the surface with icing sugar and cut slices crossways to serve.

34. Quick Hot Stew.

Slice 1 onion into
enough water to cover. Simmer for 5 mins
add any beef gravy or extract.
Season well; slice thin cold cooked
meat and drop into boiling just
before serving. With or without toast.

This was plainly a way of stretching a small amount of leftover cooked beef to make a meal for several people, and more of a guideline than a recipe because so much depends on how much leftover beef you have, and on the quality, thickness, and volume of leftover gravy.

If you have leftover beef but no leftover gravy, make a beef-flavoured sauce from beef stock thickened with a little flour—about 2 tablespoons of flour per 1 cup of beef stock. Season to taste and simmer for 15 minutes.

This makes a main meal for four if accompanied generously with potatoes and vegetables. Or, as Mrs. Ayre indicates, eat it with or on toast as a lunch or light meal. The version below is on toast.

QUICK HOT STEW
serves 4

1 medium (5 oz/150 g) onion
½ cup (125 ml) water, approximately
¼ teaspoon (1.5 g) salt
¾ cup (190 ml) beef gravy
1 cup (125 g) leftover cooked beef
4 slices of bread for toast
butter for the toast

    Chop the onion and put it in a small saucepan with enough water to almost cover. Bring to a boil, then simmer for 5 minutes with the lid half off. After 5 minutes, much of the water will have evaporated and the onion will be cooked. Add the gravy and simmer for a few minutes. Taste and adjust the seasoning. Slice the beef thinly and add it to the pot. Simmer briefly, then taste and adjust the seasoning. Toast and butter the bread. Divide the beef mixture between the slices of toast—a generous ⅓ cup on each—and serve immediately.

---

35 Quick cheese fondue.

Pour on
1 cup diced bread 1 cup milk 1 teasp
salt yolks 4 eggs and 1 cup ground
cheese   stir well, beat whites of
eggs very stiff & fold in, bake
15 – 20 mins. Serve at once.

Mrs. Ayre must have called this a fondue because of its combination of bread cubes and cheese, but it seems to have far more in common with a souffled omelette.
    It is tricky to know what is meant by diced—in this case, bread. Here smaller rather than larger dice work better because they soak up the yolk-milk mixture more quickly and make it less sloppy. One-quarter-inch cubes were about right, but don't get too fussy. The cheese adds significantly to the saltiness of this dish, so the 1 teaspoon in

her recipe makes the fondue too salty; this is reduced in our recipe below, but that can be further reduced if desired. The yolk-milk-bread-cheese mixture is sloppy, even with small cubes, so folding in the whipped egg whites is not as simple as when folding into a thicker sauce.

The finished dish is surprisingly good—but then the combination of eggs and cheese can never go too far wrong.

QUICK CHEESE FONDUE
serves 3 or 4

4 eggs
1 cup (250 ml) milk
½ teaspoon (3.3 g) salt
1 cup (75 g) grated cheese
1 cup (40 g) small cubes of bread; about one thick slice with crusts removed

Preheat the oven to 400°F. Separate the yolks and whites of the eggs. Whisk together the yolks, milk, and salt, then mix in the bread cubes and leave them to soak for 2 or 3 minutes. Then stir in the grated cheese. Whip the egg whites to stiff peaks and fold gently into the yolk-cheese mixture. Immediately pour into an 8 by 8-inch baking dish and bake about 25 minutes, or until the top is well browned. Serve immediately as a light meal.

36. Apple Chutney.

4 lbs chopped
apples, 2 lbs brown sugar   1⅓ lbs raisins
1 oz garlic, 1 oz ground ginger
2 oz mustard seed, 1 oz salt, 3 pints
vinegar. Boil like jam.

Does Mrs. Ayre mean 4 pounds of whole apples or 4 pounds after peeling and coring? Most recipes of the period dealt in the former, so we stuck with that. After you have peeled and cored the apples, don't get too fussy when cutting them up—just make sure the pieces are roughly the same size. Some apples will break down completely when cooked, to make a chutney the consistency of thick applesauce. Others are more resistant and pieces of apple will remain in the finished product.

Fresh garlic was rare, so perhaps she meant powdered garlic? Her specification of 1 ounce, like the other ground spices, indicates a dry powder, so we used garlic powder.

The instruction "Boil like jam" is a masterpiece of brevity, but covers a multitude of sins. She probably did not mean boil until it sets like jam, because chutneys are not usually jellied. The objective here was probably to boil the mixture until thick enough not to run off a spoon, which can be achieved by simmering on a low heat until reduced to about 80 per cent of its original volume. If you cannot estimate that by eye, place a ruler in the mix before simmering, and then check it at intervals afterwards.

This recipe fills about six 2-cup Mason jars to the shoulders, full enough if sterilizing them in a water bath. It is a pleasant but undistinguished chutney, good for a cheese sandwich, for example.

APPLE CHUTNEY
makes about 10 cups (2.5 l)

4 pounds (1800 g, untrimmed weight) apples, about 14 medium
6 cups (900 g) brown sugar
4 cups (600 g) raisins
3 tablespoons (30 g) garlic powder
5½ tablespoons (30 g) ground ginger
5 tablespoons (60 g) whole mustard seed
4½ teaspoons (30 g) salt
6 cups (1500 ml) vinegar

Peel and core the apples and cut into roughly ¾-inch chunks. Put all ingredients in a non-reactive (e.g., stainless steel) saucepan and bring to a boil. Simmer the mixture with the lid off until thickened to your taste (but remember that it will be a lot thicker when cold). A 20 per cent reduction in volume is about right.

37. Marshmallow cake.

Cream ⅓ cup
butter gradually beat in 1 cup sugar
Sift 2 ½ teasp baking powder with
1¼ cup flour & ½ cornstarch add
alternately to creamed mixture
with ½ cup milk   1 teasp of flavouring
& 3 stiff whites of eggs.

Looks straightforward, but there's a major snag: after the flour, cornstarch, and milk are beaten into the creamed butter and sugar, the result is so stiff that it is impossible to fold in the beaten egg whites. The mixture needs about an extra 6 tablespoons of milk to make a thick but flexible batter that can be folded into the beaten egg whites without deflating them excessively.

In the absence of other instructions, and because it is called a cake, we baked the mixture in a standard 8-inch cake pan. And because it is called a marshmallow cake, we assumed that the next recipe for marshmallow icing belongs with this one.

This cake is a perfectly good white cake (white in the sense of no yolks) and not too sweet, so it carries the sugary icing well.

MARSHMALLOW CAKE
makes one 8-inch (20 cm) cake

⅓ cup (75 g) room-temperature butter
1 cup (200 g) sugar
½ cup (60 g) corn flour
1¼ cups (190 g) flour
2½ teaspoons (12.5 g) baking powder
14 tablespoons (210 ml) milk
3 egg whites

Preheat the oven to 350°F. Grease and flour an 8-inch round cake pan. Cream together the butter and sugar. Mix the flour, cornstarch, and baking powder well. Beat this in portions into the creamed butter and sugar, alternating with milk. Whisk the egg whites to stiff peaks and fold into the batter. Pour and scrape this mixture into the prepared cake pan. Bake about 50 to 60 minutes, or until a small skewer pushed into the thickest part comes out clean. Turn out onto a rack and leave to cool while making the icing (next recipe).

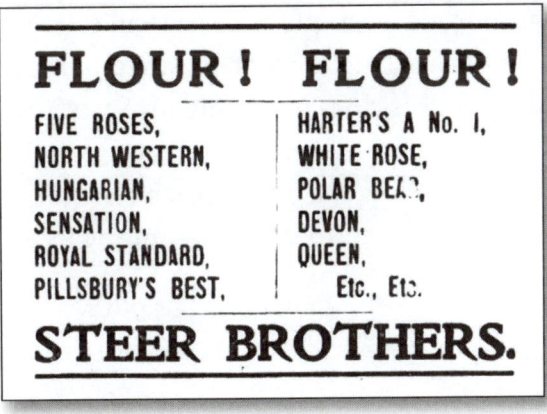

Evening Telegram, January 24, 1902.

38 Icing.

Heat 2 tablesp milk with 6 tablesp sugar over fire Boil 6 mins without stirring. In double boiler heat ¼ lb cut marshmallows. When very soft add 2 tablesp boiling water & cook till smooth. Beat in hot sugar. Keep beating till partly cool. ½ teasp vanilla.

It is always tricky using simple timing as a guide when boiling sugar and milk (or water) to produce a hot syrup. But in this case, where we think she was aiming for the soft-ball stage in fact 6 minutes of boiling always seemed to be about right in our numerous attempts. Use a small candy thermometer to make sure.

Her instruction not to stir is aimed at avoiding crystallization of the mixture, although this does not really apply at these relatively low temperatures.

The icing is suitably sweet for the above cake. A minor problem is that the melted marshmallow makes it rather viscous, so it sticks to the knife when cutting the cake; the knife will need frequent wiping.

ICING
makes enough for one cake

6 tablespoons (75 g) sugar
2 tablespoons (30 ml) milk
3 cups (110 g) marshmallows
2 tablespoons (30 ml) boiling water

If the marshmallows are large, cut them into smaller pieces, about ½-inch cubes. Put the marshmallows in a bowl set over simmering water and heat until they start to melt in places. Add the boiling water and stir the mixture until the marshmallows are all melted and the mixture is completely smooth. Bring the milk and sugar to a boil in a small saucepan and simmer about 6 minutes, or until it reaches the soft-ball stage. While stirring vigorously, pour this onto the melted marshmallow. When the mixture is completely homogeneous, take it off the heat and let it cool, stirring occasionally.

When both cake and icing are completely cool, pour and scrape the icing onto the centre of the cake. Gently smooth the icing over the top of the cake using circular motions with the back of a spoon. It will flow reluctantly, so nudge it toward the edge of the cake, and if it does drip down the sides in places, that looks rather attractive.

39 Gingerbread

1 cup molasses 1 cup brown sugar add 1 cup shortening & 1 teasp cinnamon, nutmeg ¼ teasp cloves 1 tablesp ground ginger. Place these in a bowl and stand in a warm place till shortening has softened. Then beat to a cream. Beat 3 eggs very light & add & stir in ½ teasp salt. Sift 3 ½ cups pastry flour with 1 teasp soda and beat into mixture alternately with a cup sour milk, buttermilk or cold water. Whip batter well & pour into well greased dripping pan & bake in a moderate oven about 40 mins
This makes large cake.

The recipe specifies shortening, so we assume she used either Crisco or Snowdrift, both available in her day (see also recipe 33). We used Crisco.

The specified pastry flour is unnecessary; the recipe works well with regular all-purpose white flour. Sifting is not necessary; it is sufficient to mix the soda into the flour because it gets plenty more mixing in the batter.

Dripping pans were shallow, rectangular pans designed to sit under spit-roasting meat to catch drippings (the fat and juices). When oven-roasting supplanted spit-roasting, the pans were put to other uses, as here. They came in different sizes, and we do not know which she had in mind, but to get the cake to cook in 40 minutes requires a pan about 10 by 16 inches. But the problem with that size is that the cake is too thin; to produce a cake of proper thickness needs a pan of about 80 square inches. Instead of a rectangular pan, we used a 10-inch round cake pan, but any pan of similar area can be used. To make loaf-shaped cakes, as befits the title Gingerbread, use two standard loaf pans, about 4 by 9 inches at the base.

It is best to both grease and flour the pan to ensure that the baked cake slips out easily.

This cake has a better flavour if made with the sour milk or buttermilk she mentions but works perfectly well with water. Either way, it makes a good, basic ginger cake, which is much improved by butter and jam.

GINGERBREAD

makes one 10-inch (25 cm) round cake or equivalent

- 1 cup (250 ml) molasses
- 1 cup (150 g) brown sugar
- 1 cup (195 g) room-temperature shortening
- 1 teaspoon (3 g) cinnamon
- ¼ teaspoon (0.75 g) nutmeg
- ¼ teaspoon (0.75 g) cloves
- 1 tablespoon (5 g) ginger
- 3 eggs
- ½ teaspoon (3.3 g) salt
- 3½ cups (525 g) flour
- 1 teaspoon (5 g) baking soda
- 1 cup (250 ml) cold water

Preheat the oven to 350°F. Grease and flour a 10-inch round cake pan. Beat together the shortening, brown sugar, molasses, and spices into a smooth cream. In a separate bowl, whisk the eggs until completely homogeneous and then whisk in the salt. Beat this mixture into the shortening-spice mixture until completely smooth. Mix the flour and baking soda well, then beat portions of this alternately with portions of water into the shortening-egg mixture. Make sure all is thoroughly mixed, then pour and scrape into the prepared pan.

Bake about 75 to 80 minutes, or until a small skewer inserted into the thickest part comes out clean.

40 Ginger Patties.

Bake in sm. patty tins & sprinkle with sugar just before it is done. When baked cakes may be slipped under flame or top of very hot oven to glaze. Just before it is finished stick halved marshmallows over the surface and return to oven until m mallows are puffy and brown.

This is a sequel to the previous recipe, giving different ways of using the same cake mixture. Patty pans were small tinware, ceramic, or glass pastry forms, typically with sloping sides and a fluted or scalloped rim. The name was applied to all sizes of such moulds, from 5- or 6-inch individual pie plates to small 2-inch moulds. We have no idea what size Mrs. Ayre used, but the principle is to bake the cake batter in small portions, so we tried a range of pans. The smallest were made in standard muffin pans, about 3 inches in diameter across the wide end and 1¼ inches deep. The largest were in shallow, 4½-inch mini-quiche pans with fluted rims, which made small, two-portion cakes.

Mrs. Ayre gives two ways of finishing these patties. The easiest is to place pieces of marshmallow on the top of the baked patty and put back in the oven to brown. The difficult one is glazing the tops with sugar, difficult because the sugar slides off the sloping rim of the domed, cooked patties, leaving the rim of the cake prone to burning under the direct heat of the broiler.

GINGER PATTIES
makes about 24 muffin-sized portions

1 recipe of gingerbread (39) **marshmallows or sugar for sprinkling**

Preheat the oven to 350°F. Grease and flour 24 standard muffin cups. Because of the molasses, this batter tends to stick, so it is important to be liberal with the greasing and flouring—it is best to grease and flour even non-stick pans. Divide the batter between the muffin cups, about ⅓ cup in each. Bake for about 20 minutes or until a small skewer inserted into the thickest part comes out clean.

These may be finished by placing small pieces of marshmallow on top of each and putting them back in the oven for about 10 minutes, or until the marshmallow pieces are puffed and browned on top. For a sugar glaze, sprinkle about ½ teaspoon of sugar over the top of each, and broil for 2 or 3 minutes, or until the sugar is melting; be careful not to let the exposed parts of the tops burn.

For larger, two-portion patties, grease and flour 10 small pans, about 4½ inches in diameter, and use about ¾ cup of batter in each. Bake about 25 to 30 minutes, or until a small skewer inserted into the thickest part comes out clean. These can be finished in the same fashion as above, with marshmallows or sugar. If using the sugar-glaze method, use about 1 teaspoon of sugar, and be careful not to burn the tops.

41 Gingernuts.

Cream ½ cup shortening
1 cup brown sugar & add well beaten
egg. Then sift 2 cups pastry
flour mixed with 1 tablesp ground
ginger ¼ teasp salt. Make dough
into little balls. Mod. oven.
Blanched almond or bit citron in each.
Gingerbread men, animals.

Pastry flour is not necessary; regular white, all-purpose flour works perfectly. Sifting can be omitted as long as the flour, ginger, and salt are thoroughly stirred together. The dough is dry and crumbly, making it awkward to handle and roll out because the edges crack and fall apart.

To divide the dough into portions, press it into a log on the counter and cut into the desired number of pieces (24 works). Roll each portion into a ball. However, if the portions are baked as spheres, as Mrs. Ayre says, they burn on the base before the centres are cooked. It is best to press each ball into a thick disk, about 2 inches in diameter and about 3/8 inch thick.

This dough makes a tough biscuit, ideal for gingerbread men and animals. For this, divide the dough into 4 portions, and roll each thinly (3/16 inch). One large gingerbread man or animal shape (or more smaller ones) can be cut from each portion. Such thinly rolled dough can also be cut into 2½-inch biscuits.

These are good, basic ginger biscuits, although they may be hard for some tastes.

GINGERNUTS
makes about 24 biscuits

1 cup (150 g) brown sugar
½ cup (95 g) shortening
1 egg

2 cups (300 g) flour
1 tablespoon (5 g) ginger
¼ teaspoon (1.5 g) salt

Garnish
either slivers of almonds or small pieces candied citron

Preheat the oven to 350°F. These biscuits will not stick to a well-seasoned baking sheet, but if you wish, line one with parchment paper or a silicone mat. Cream together the brown sugar and shortening. Beat in the egg. Mix the flour, ginger, and salt, then mix thoroughly with the sugar mixture. Turn out onto the counter, and press the mixture together to make the dough hold together in a log. Cut into 24 pieces. Roll each portion into a ball. Put each ball on the counter and press it gently into a fat disk about 2 inches in diameter. The rim will crumble and split, so gently push the edges back into the disk to make a more or less tidy circle. Using a thin metal spatula, transfer the disks to the baking sheet. As they do not spread much during baking, they can be close together. Bake for about 20 minutes, or until the tops are lightly browned

42 Cream Dressing

> 1 teasp mustard   1 teasp salt   2 teasp flour
> 3 teasp sugar   ½ t pepper   1 teasp
> melted butter   yolk 1 egg   1 tablesp
> vinegar   ½ cup thick cream

Apart from the real mayonnaise that was made domestically in her day (see recipe 7), several pseudo-mayonnaise concoctions were available commercially, such as Durkee's, Libby's, and Premier salad dressing. Those brands no longer exist. Imitation mayonnaises are to be avoided, however, and this one is no exception.

CREAM DRESSING
makes about 1¼ cups (310 ml)

1 teaspoon (3 g) dry mustard
1 teaspoon (6.5 g) salt
2 teaspoons (6.5 g) flour
1 tablespoon (12.5 g) sugar
1 teaspoon (5 g) melted butter
1 tablespoon (15 ml) vinegar
1 egg yolk
½ cup (125 ml) cream

Place a bowl over a saucepan of barely simmering water. Put the butter in the bowl and let it melt. Mix together the mustard, salt, flour, and sugar. Stir this mixture into the melted butter to make a crumbly paste. Stir in the vinegar to make a smooth paste. Mix in the egg yolk and stir over the simmering water until the mixture thickens to a stiff paste. Take the bowl off the heat and leave to cool (stand it in cold water to speed this up). Whip the cream to stiff peaks and fold into the cooled mixture.

43 Pineapple Cream

> yolks 3 eggs ½ cup pineapple juice
> ½ cup sugar. Make into a custard
> 3 sheets gelatine soaked in a little juice
> add to custard. Cut up ½ or ¾ tin
> chunks. Whip ½ pt. cream & whites
> of 3 eggs separately, & when whipped
> beat together. When custard is cold
> add to cream and whites.

Do not be tempted to use fresh pineapple in this recipe, because its enzymes will degrade the gelatine. Use canned chunks and some of the juice—the enzymes have been destroyed by heating. The standard sizes of cans were 1 pound and ½ pound. Mrs. Ayre calls for one-half or three-quarters of a can of pineapple, and we found that about three-quarters of a 14-ounce can was about right, that is, about 7 ounces drained weight pineapple.

Sheet gelatine was (and is) more used in Europe than in North America, so she may have picked up this recipe from a British source. Opinions differ, but a useful conversion is that 1 tablespoon of granular gelatine is equivalent to 3 sheets of gelatine.

If you are not accustomed to custard, use a small instant-read thermometer and cook it to about 176°F. Let the custard cool before you whip the egg whites and cream.

PINEAPPLE CREAM
serves 6

1 tablespoon (10 g) granular gelatine
3 tablespoons (45 ml) canned
    pineapple juice
3 eggs

½ cup (125 ml) canned pineapple juice
½ cup (100 g) sugar
1¼ cups (200 g) canned pineapple cubes
1 cup (250 ml) cream

Put the 3 tablespoons of pineapple juice in a small, wide, shallow dish and sprinkle the gelatine over the surface. Soak for about 5 minutes. Whisk the egg yolks, cream, and ½ cup of pineapple juice in a bowl set over simmering water, and continue whisking until a thin custard has formed. Cool (it can be set in a sink of cold water to speed up the cooling; if it cools too much and sets before you are ready for it, warm it briefly over warm water). Cut the drained pineapple into ½-inch cubes and reserve. When the custard has cooled and become like a thick syrup, whisk separately to stiff peaks both the egg whites and the cream. Fold these together, and then fold in the custard. When they are well combined, fold in the reserved pineapple chunks. Divide the mixture between 6 wide dessert glasses, about ¾ cup in each.

44 Marmalade (Orange)

9 oranges or 12
3 lemons, 7 lbs sugar   1 gal water.
Soak 36 hours in water   Boil 1 ¼ hrs
without sugar. Add sugar & boil
another   hour.

The choice between nine or 12 oranges was likely the choice between larger or smaller fruit. The oranges we used were large, each around 8 ounces, so we made this recipe with 9 oranges. Seedless varieties of both fruit reduce the work involved. If you are nervous about residual pesticides on the oranges and lemons, scrub them with warm soapy water and rinse thoroughly before proceeding.

If you like thin-cut marmalade, sliver the fruit as thinly as you can. If thick-cut is your preference, slice the fruit nearly ¼ inch thick. Kitchen mandolins are not very useful here—they crush, rather than slice, the fruit. Without a very fancy slicing machine, cut the fruit by hand. Sharpen the knife, lay 2 quarters of a fruit peel-side up on the cutting board, and start slicing across the short axis from one end. Toward the other end the fruit will become unstable (because it is now taller than it is wide), so turn it on its side and continue slicing.

Soaking the slivered fruit for varying lengths of time was a characteristic of marmalade recipes of the period. It supposedly reduced the bitterness of the finished product, but we found little difference when the soaking was omitted. But to be faithful to Mrs. Ayre, the fruit was soaked for 36 hours.

Cooking any jam or marmalade according to a time is not a good idea. This batch, for example, took about 1 hour and 45 minutes after the sugar was added to reach the setting temperature (220°F). Use a candy thermometer (or other method of determining setting point—see any standard work on jam-making). This recipe makes an excellent, tasty marmalade, enough to fill twelve 2-cup Mason jars to the shoulder.

MARMALADE (ORANGE)
makes about 20 cups (4.8 l)

9 large (about 2.025 kg, total untrimmed weight) oranges
3 (about 500 g, total weight) lemons

1 gallon (3.8 l) water
7 pounds (3.2 kg) sugar

Put the water in the non-reactive pot you will use to boil the marmalade. Cut out the little stem sockets. Cut the fruit in half and pick out all visible seeds. Cut each half in half and check for more seeds. Sliver all the fruit, checking for more seeds. Mix the slivered fruit with the water in the pot and leave for 36 hours, stirring occasionally. Then bring the mixture to a boil, and simmer it for 75 minutes with the lid on. Add the sugar, bring it back to a boil, and simmer another 1 or 2 hours, or until the setting point is reached (220°F). Ladle the finished marmalade into Mason jars and cool.

Evening Telegram, January 29, 1918.

Pickavance & Murphy

> ## 45 Date + walnut cake
>
> 1 lb. dates, ¾ cup sugar ½ cup flour
> 1 teasp baking powder   ½ lb walnuts
> 3 eggs – separate.

A dauntingly brief recipe even for experienced bakers—a real problem for the rest of us. And there is a problem: the yolk, flour, and sugar mixture is too thick to fold with the whipped egg whites. It needs a few tablespoons of milk to make it soft enough to fold.

Dates came whole or pitted, and in terms of quantity it does not matter which you use (as long as you remove the pits). The dates were chopped roughly by hand, until there was no piece bigger than about ½ inch. The nuts were coarsely chopped to pieces about the same as the dates.

Pecans were used in testing this recipe. The completed batter is copious, so use a deep 3 by 8-inch cake pan or a regular 9-inch pan. This makes a dense but pleasant cake.

DATE & WALNUT CAKE
makes one 8 or 9-inch (20 or 23 cm) cake

3 eggs, separated
¾ cup (150 g) sugar
½ cup (75 g) flour
1 teaspoon (5 g) baking powder

2–3 tablespoons (30–45 ml) milk
4 cups (450 g) dates
2¼ cups (225 g) walnuts or pecans

Preheat the oven to 350°F. Grease and flour a deep 8-inch cake pan (or a regular 9-inch pan). Coarsely chop the dates and nuts. Beat the yolks and sugar together. Mix the flour and baking powder together. Beat the flour mixture into the yolk mixture, alternating with milk to make a loose batter. Whip the egg whites to stiff peaks and fold gently into the batter. Then fold in the chopped dates and nuts, and pour and scrape this into the prepared pan.

Bake 60 minutes, or until a small skewer inserted in the thickest part comes out clean. A 9-inch cake will take about 50 minutes. Turn out on a rack and cool.

46 Potato Cakes

4 cups hot mashed potatoes, ½ cup butter 1 teasp baking powder & enough flour to mix & bind. Roll and cut in round cakes. Bake in oven for 15 or 20 minutes eat hot with butter.

To get 4 cups of mashed potato, start with about 2½ pounds whole unpeeled potatoes.

This recipe is much easier with hot freshly mashed potato. But cold leftover potato will still work as long as the butter is very soft so that it will mix thoroughly with it. This recipe needs a little salt and pepper.

The amount of flour specified below makes a loose, soft dough that is tricky to handle; add more flour to make a stiffer dough if you prefer. Although the dough is conveniently rolled out in our method, it can equally well be flattened by hand.

The size of the potato cakes is not specified, and is a matter of taste. These are fine potato cakes, good as the starch with a meal.

POTATO CAKES
makes 12 cakes

4 cups (800 g) mashed potato
½ cup (110 g) butter
1 teaspoon (5 g) baking powder

12 tablespoons (120 g) flour
½ teaspoon (3.3 g) salt
½ teaspoon (1.5 g) pepper

Preheat the oven to 350°F. Mix the mashed potato well with the butter, baking powder, salt, and pepper. Mix in portions of flour until the mixture binds together. Roll or press the potato dough to about ¾ inch thick on a lightly floured surface, which makes an 8 to 9-inch circle. Cut out 3-inch circles with a cookie cutter. Re-roll the scraps and cut out more circles, to make about 12 in all. Pick up the circles carefully with a thin-bladed spatula. Place these on a lightly greased baking sheet (or parchment paper or a silicone mat). Bake 30 to 40 minutes, or until the undersides are lightly browned. These cakes do not set but spread slightly and puff up after about 30 minutes. Serve with extra butter if desired.

47 Orange Jelly

2 tablesp gelatine
½ cup cold water ½ cup sugar
½ cup boiling water 3 tablesp lemon
juice, 1 cup orange juice
Soak gelatine 5 mins in cold water
dissolve in boiling water, add sugar
sunkist orange & lemon juice & strain into
a mold. Put in a cold place to
stiffen Cut in cubes, serve in orange
baskets or half orange skins cut
into points
[in the notebook, there are two little drawings here: half an orange with jagged rim; an orange basket with a handle]

Granular gelatine is the typical form in North America, so Mrs. Ayre likely picked up this recipe from a Canadian or American source (see also recipe 43). Once the gelatine has absorbed the cold water, add the hot water to dissolve the gelatine completely before adding the juices. Mrs. Ayre likely used Sunkist oranges (and possibly lemons)—Sunkist was a leading brand of Californian citrus fruit in her time. To get the required volume of orange juice, we squeezed an extra orange over and above those needed to makes the containers.

From the amount of jelly this recipe makes, we filled 6 baskets or 8 cups carved from large oranges, about 8 ounces each, with diameters around 3 inches.

Straining the juice-gelatine mixture before chilling is not necessary unless there are too many pits in the juice.

This makes a cheerful dessert. Perhaps better suited to a children's birthday party than an adult dinner, although we must confess to a sneaking fondness for fruit jelly—real homemade fruit jelly that is, not the commercial packaged stuff.

ORANGE JELLY
makes 6 to 8 orange cups

2 tablespoons (20 g) gelatine
½ cup (125 ml) cold water
½ cup (125 ml) boiling water
½ cup (100 g) sugar
1 cup (250 ml) orange juice, from 4–6 oranges
3 tablespoons (45 ml) lemon juice, from 1 lemon

Put the cold water in a wide bowl, sprinkle the gelatine evenly over it, and let it soak about 5 minutes. Add the boiling water and stir until all the gelatine is dissolved. Stir in the sugar, lemon juice, and orange juice. Stir until the sugar has completely dissolved. Strain this mixture into an 8 by 8-inch or other convenient size pan. Refrigerate until well set. Cut the jelly into around ¾-inch cubes. Divide the jelly cubes between about 6 orange-rind baskets, or about 8 jagged-edge half-oranges.

To make half-orange containers, cut in a zigzag fashion around the equator of the orange (the stem and blossom ends being the poles) with a small, sharp knife. Drive the knife to at least the centre of the orange so that the two halves pull apart easily when you have cut all the way around. Squeeze the juice out of each half. Then use a melon baller or small spoon to scrape the membranes from the white pith. Scrape and pull the membranes until the pith is completely clean. Trim a thin sliver off each end of each half-orange so that it will stand on a plate without wobbling. Reserve until needed.

To make orange baskets, trim a thin sliver off the stem end of the orange so that it will stand on a plate without wobbling. Make two cuts straight down from the other end, about ⅜ inch apart. Cut down as far as the equator to form the handle of the basket. Then turn the knife horizontally, and cut around the equator to join the vertical cut on the other side.

Remove the segment of orange. Repeat this on the other side of the handle. Squeeze out as much juice as possible, taking care not to break the handle. Scrape out the membranes as described above.

48 Spice Cake

1 cup sugar ½ cup butter
1 cup sour milk   yolk 1 egg ½ teasp
cloves 1 cup raisins 2¼ cups flour
1 teasp soda ½ teasp cinnamon.
Bake in loaves & frost with boiled
frosting – 1 cup sugar ½ teasp cream tartar
white 1 egg flavour lemon.
Beat egg white stiff & add 1 tablesp
sugar & cream of tartar. Put rest
of sugar & little water on stove & boil
until syrup threads – then pour on
egg & beat until ready to spread on
cake & flavour.

Because this is a soda-leavened cake, some acid in the batter is needed to activate the soda. Mrs. Ayre used sour milk. Milk these days does not go gracefully sour like it used to, but gets a rather unpleasant fermented edge to it. We recommend using buttermilk instead. However, be careful, because some buttermilks are not acidic enough. Taste it before using, and add 1 teaspoon of vinegar as an insurance if it does not have a pronounced acidity. If you have neither sour milk nor buttermilk, use plain milk with 1 teaspoon of vinegar.

To faithfully follow Mrs. Ayre's recipe, bake the batter in 2 small loaf pans, about 4 by 7 inches. We baked it as one 8-inch cake. For the frosting, the thread stage Mrs. Ayre mentions is really not hot enough to make a stable, meringue-style frosting. It needs to be boiled to the soft-ball stage, as explained below.

A pleasant, lightly spiced cake but on the dry side, so wash it down with a mug of tea as an afternoon snack.

SPICE CAKE
makes one 8-inch (20 cm) cake

1 cup (200 g) sugar
½ cup (110 g) butter
1 egg yolk
½ teaspoon (1.5 g) cloves
½ teaspoon (1.5 g) cinnamon

2¼ cups (340 g) flour
1 teaspoon (5 g) baking soda
1 cup (250 ml) buttermilk
1 teaspoon (5 ml) vinegar, if necessary

Frosting

1 cup (200 g) sugar
3 tablespoons (45 ml) water
1 egg white

½ teaspoon (1.5 g) cream of tartar
½ teaspoon (2.5 ml) lemon essence

Preheat the oven to 350°F. Grease and flour an 8-inch cake pan. Separate the egg. Beat the sugar with the butter until pale, then beat in the yolk, cloves, and cinnamon. Mix the baking soda with the flour, then beat portions of this into the sugar-butter mixture alternately with buttermilk. When it is well mixed, scrape and pour the batter into the prepared pan and bake 50 minutes, or until a small skewer pushed into the thickest part comes out clean.

While the cake is baking, make the frosting. Take 1 tablespoon of sugar out of the 1 cup of sugar and reserve. Put the rest of the sugar in a small saucepan with the water and bring to a boil. While the sugar is boiling, whip the egg white to soft peaks, then whip in the tartar and the 1 tablespoon of sugar to firm peaks. When the sugar has reached the soft-ball stage, pour it slowly onto the whipped egg white, beating continuously. Continue beating for about 5 minutes after all the sugar syrup has been added, until the mixture has cooled and thickened considerably. Beat in the lemon essence and set aside to cool more. When the cake has cooled, spread the frosting over the top and sides of the cake.

49 Chocolate Fudge

3 cups sugar, 2 sq chocolate ½ cup milk   butter size egg   2 tablesp molasses. Mix ingredients & boil six minutes stirring constantly Remove from stove add 1 teasp vanilla & beat until begins to grain.

Six minutes at a rapid boil to get to the soft-ball stage is about right (see recipe 38), but time is a notoriously unreliable guide when boiling sugar, and there is no excuse for not using a candy thermometer. So as Mrs. Ayre suggests in a previous fudge recipe (11), boil the mixture to the soft-ball stage. For the chocolate, we used semi-sweet baking chocolate, but any chocolate works well.

CHOCOLATE FUDGE
makes about 64 pieces

3 cups (600 g) sugar
½ cup (125 ml) milk
2 squares (60 g) chocolate
¼ cup (50 g) butter
2 tablespoons (30 ml) molasses
1 teaspoon (5 ml) vanilla

Put all the ingredients except the vanilla in a small saucepan and bring to a boil. Boil the mixture about 6 minutes, or until it reaches the soft-ball stage. Take the saucepan off the heat, add the vanilla, and stir it intermittently as it cools. After approximately 20 to 30 minutes, it will get noticeably thicker as it starts to crystallize. Pour and scrape it into an 8 by 8-inch shallow pan and cool.

50 Sponge Cake.

4 eggs ⅔ cup sugar
⅔ cup flour ⅔ tablesp lemon juice
grated rind of ⅙ lemon ¼ teasp salt
Beat yolks eggs until thick &
creamy & add sugar a little at a
time beating with egg beater.
Add lemon juice & grated rind &
then stiff whites. When whites are
partly mixed with yolks & sugar
add flour mixed & sifted with
salt cutting and folding it into
the mixture. Bake one hour
over a low flame using a long
narrow pan.

Where did Mrs. Ayre get this recipe, with its spuriously precise ingredient of the zest of one-sixth of a lemon? In practice in the kitchen, one-quarter of a lemon is easier to estimate, which is what we used here.

Unlike recipe 48, where she says bake in loaves and we used a round cake pan, this time we followed her recommendation and used a long loaf pan, but this will work equally well in a regular 8-inch round cake pan. This makes a good basic sponge cake that lends itself to any kind of garnish.

SPONGE CAKE
makes one loaf

4 eggs
⅔ cup (135 g) sugar
⅔ cup (100 g) flour

2 teaspoons (10 ml) lemon juice
zest of ¼ lemon
¼ teaspoon (1.5 g) salt

Preheat the oven to 350°F. Grease and flour a 4½ by 11½-inch loaf pan. Separate the eggs. Beat the yolks until pale yellow and thick. Beat in the sugar. Mix in the lemon juice and zest. Whip the egg whites to stiff peaks. Mix the salt and flour. Fold the whipped whites and the flour mixture alternately into the butter-sugar mixture until well mixed together. Pour and scrape into the prepared pan and bake 30 to 35 minutes, or until a small skewer inserted into the thickest part comes out clean. Turn out on a rack to cool.

51 Currant Cake

½ cup butter   1 cup sugar
2 eggs   yolk 1 egg   ½ cup milk
2 cups flour   3 teasp baking powder
2 cups currants mixed 1 tablsp flour
Cream butter add sugar eggs & egg yolk well beaten   milk flour mixed & sifted with baking powder & currants   Bake forty minutes

This makes a very pleasant currant cake, well suited to afternoon tea.

CURRANT CAKE
makes one 8-inch (23 cm) round cake

½ cup (110 g) butter
1 cup (200 g) sugar
2 eggs
1 egg yolk
½ cup (125 ml) milk

2 cups (300 g) flour
3 teaspoons (15 g) baking powder
2 cups (300 g) currants
1 tablespoon (10 g) flour

Preheat the oven to 350°F. Grease and flour an 8-inch cake pan. Beat the butter and sugar together until pale and fluffy. Beat in the eggs and yolk. Mix the 2 cups of flour with the baking powder, and stir into the butter-sugar mixture. Mix the 1 tablespoon of flour with the currants until they are well coated, and stir this in. Pour and scrape the mixture into the prepared pan and bake 55 to 60 minutes, or until a small skewer inserted into the thickest part comes out clean. Turn out on a rack to cool.

---

52 Chocolate Cake

1 ¼ cups sugar   ½ cup butter   2 eggs   2 cups flour
1 teasp soda   2 teasps cream of tartar
1 cup milk   3 small tablesps cocoa
1 teasp vanilla. Cream butter add sugar whites of eggs beaten stiff yolk eggs beaten. Milk   flour cocoa cream tartar & soda mixed & sifted together   & vanilla. Boiled icing

---

Mrs. Ayre's method is confusing because she wants the egg whites whipped, presumably to add lift to the cake, but then appears to add them in the middle of the process, which would deflate them almost totally. We suggest folding in the whipped whites at the end. When doing so, lighten the flour mixture with a small portion of the whipped whites before folding in the rest.

CHOCOLATE CAKE
makes one 8-inch (23 cm) round cake

1¼ cups (250 g) sugar
½ cup (110 g) butter
2 eggs
2 cups (300 g) flour
1 teaspoon (5 g) baking soda

2 teaspoons (10 g) cream of tartar
1 cup (250 ml) milk
3 tablespoons (23 g) cocoa
1 teaspoon (5 ml) vanilla
boiled icing (see recipe 48)

Preheat the oven to 350°F. Grease and flour a 3-inch-deep, 8-inch cake pan. Separate the eggs. Cream together the butter and sugar. Beat in the yolks, cocoa, vanilla, and milk. Mix the flour, baking soda, and cream of tartar and beat into the mixture. Whip the egg whites to stiff peaks. Stir about ½ cup of the whipped whites into the mixture first to lighten it, then fold in the remainder. Pour and scrape this mixture into the prepared pan and bake 55 to 60 minutes, or until a small skewer inserted into the thickest part comes out clean. Turn out on a rack to cool. Make boiled icing (recipe 48). When both cake and icing are cool, spread the icing over the top and sides of the cake.

VAN HOUTEN'S COCOA

GOLD LABEL · BROWN LABEL

Two flavors for different palates.
Pure · Soluble · Delicious.
ALL GOOD-CLASS STORES SELL IT.

Evening Telegram, June 3, 1925.

53 Rhubarb Pudding

2 cups flour
½ teasp salt   3 tablesp baking powder
6 tablesp brown sugar   1½ lbs rhubarb
½ cup butter   ½ lemon   ½ cup white sugar

Brown the white sugar in a saucepan & coat the inside of buttered mould with it   Sift flour baking powder & salt   work in butter & mix to consistency of biscuit dough with cold water. Reserve ⅓ for top. Roll out the remainder & line mould with it. Fill rhubarb cut finely add grated rind & juice of lemon, brown sugar & three tablesp of water   Roll out the pastry for top wet the edges & place it. Cover with a buttered paper and bake 1 hour. Use medium flame.

Mrs. Ayre calls this a pudding, so we recommend a pudding basin, about 8 to 10 cups capacity, about 7½ inches at the open end and about 5 inches tall, but the recipe can be adapted to other sizes of basin or mould.

Browning the sugar is now usually called caramelizing. This can be tricky unless you are used to making dishes that call for it, like crème caramel. A few pointers: put 2 tablespoons of water in a small saucepan (6 cups); pour the ½ cup of sugar in the middle of this; bring to a boil and then simmer on a low heat for about 15 to 20 minutes. Do not stir the mixture; give the saucepan at most a few gentle swirls to mix it up. If the liquid seizes up (crystallizes into a solid mass), discard and start again. Stirring increases the risk of the sugar crystallizing on the sides of the pot, which can precipitate crystallization of the whole mass. However, the liquid sugar will usually form a skim of crystals on its surface, so that bubbles look like they are covered in ice—but just carry on until the molten sugar gets to pale amber. At that point it must be watched very carefully. As soon as the sugar verges on dark amber and starts to smoke slightly, take it off the heat and pour into the pudding basin. Tip and rotate the basin to swirl the liquid caramel about half or two-thirds way up the sides. This amber, liquid caramel is extremely hot, around 360°F, and can cause a serious burn if you are careless.

If you have repeated failures—if the sugar seizes up every time—try adding 1 teaspoon of corn syrup to the initial mixture, which helps prevent crystallization.

Mrs. Ayre says to grease the pudding basin, but this is not a good idea, because the liquid caramel will not stick to the sides of the basin but instead slumps to the bottom.

Make the dough as any other pastry: either rub the butter into the flour between the tips of thumbs and fingers, or cut it in with a multi-bladed dough blender. Either way, the pieces of butter should be no bigger than a split pea. Do not add all the water at once—start with about 8 tablespoons, adding more as needed to just get the dough to hold together. Wrap the pastry in plastic film and place it in the refrigerator for 1 hour to let it relax.

Specifying how thick to roll pastry is always tricky; it is much easier to specify a two-dimensional size: in this case, rolling the two-thirds portion to a 14-inch circle is about right. Roll the other one-third of the pastry to about a 9- to 10-inch circle.

Normally a pudding is steamed, but in this case it is baked as per Mrs. Ayre's instruction. The circle of buttered (or parchment) paper will make sure that the top of the pastry does not overcook, but is not necessary. The hour that is mentioned is insufficient; cook for 75 minutes or more, until the juices bubble up at the rim. Turn out on a serving plate: invert a plate on top of the cooked pudding, then flip the whole thing over, and carefully lift off the basin.

RHUBARB PUDDING
serves at least 8

½ cup (100 g) sugar   2 tablespoons (30 ml) water

2 cups (300 g) flour   3 tablespoons (45 g) baking powder
½ cup (110 g) butter   8–10 tablespoons (120–150 ml)
½ teaspoon (3.3 g) salt   cold water

6 tablespoons (55 g) brown sugar   ½ lemon
6 cups (675 g) rhubarb   3 tablespoons (45 ml) water

Melt the ½ cup sugar with 2 tablespoons of water and heat gently until it has turned a dark amber colour. Pour into an 8 to 10-cup pudding basin, then tip and rotate the basin to swirl the liquid caramel about half or two-thirds way up the sides. Put aside to cool.

Mix the flour, salt, and baking powder, then rub or cut in the butter. Stir in enough of the cold water to just hold the dough together. Refrigerate 1 hour. Roll out two-thirds of the dough to about a 14-inch circle. Carefully pick it up on a rolling pin and gently push into the caramel-coated pudding basin. If using the recommended basin, it should come very close to the top rim. Fold and pleat the pastry as necessary up the sides of the basin.

Preheat the oven to 325°F. Remove the zest from half a lemon and squeeze out the juice. Slice the rhubarb thinly and toss with the zest, lemon juice, brown sugar, and the 3 tablespoons of water. Place in the pastry-lined basin, wet the top edge of the pastry in the basin, and lay the lid piece on top. Press the lid firmly against the rhubarb, then crimp the two layers of pastry together with your fingers, or press the tines of a fork into them, pressing them against the side of the basin. When they are well stuck together, run a small, sharp knife around the inside of the basin to cut off the ragged edge of the pastry.

Bake for about 75 minutes, or until the juices bubble up at the top. Turn out on a serving plate, cut portions, and spoon a little of the juices that will accumulate on the plate onto each portion.

54 Strawberry Sauce.

1 cup powdered sugar, white one egg, ⅔ cup straw berries, ⅓ cup butter

Cream butter and sugar, egg beaten stiff & mashed berries. Beat thoroughly

Powdered sugar is likely either the very finely powdered sugar called caster sugar in Britain or icing sugar. The recipe will work with regular sugar, however, if it is thoroughly beaten with the butter and strawberries to totally dissolve it. When measuring the volume of strawberries, chop them coarsely into ½-inch chunks before packing lightly into a cup measure.

If you are using fresh strawberries that are meltingly soft and ripe, mash them with a fork. But most modern, commercial strawberries are difficult to mash because they are bred for keeping and transportation qualities, not for soft juiciness. In which case, use a food processor to completely mix the butter, sugar, and strawberries.

The egg white, whipped to lighten the sauce, should be folded in last.

This is a thick sauce, like whipped cream. Since there is no indication of what this sauce was intended for, it was presumably a general-purpose sauce. It works well spooned over portions of sponge cake (recipe 50) or ice cream. Its quality depends entirely on the quality of the strawberries; try to make this only when fresh, flavourful local strawberries are in season.

STRAWBERRY SAUCE
makes about 2 cups (500 ml)

1 cup (120 g) icing sugar, or 1 cup (200 g) regular granular sugar
⅓ cup (75 g) butter
⅔ cup (135 g) strawberries
1 egg white

Cream the butter and ½ cup of sugar together. Mash the strawberries and then beat them into the sugar and butter. Alternatively, process butter, sugar, and berries until they are homogeneous. Whip the egg whites to stiff peaks with the other ½ cup of sugar, and fold with the strawberry mixture.

---

55 Boiled Custard.

1 pint hot milk
yolks 3 eggs   ¼ cup sugar   ⅛ teasp
salt, ½ teasp vanilla or orange.
Beat eggs a little add sugar & salt
& then hot milk stirring constantly
cook in a double boiler until mixture
thickens & a coating forms on spoon
stirring all the time   Strain cool & flavour
Should custard curdle beat with a
[another?] egg – beaten until smooth.

Traditionally, the word *boiled* meant anything from a full boil to something well below the boiling point, as here. Making custard in a double boiler is still one of the easiest methods. If you are unfamiliar with the criterion of coating a spoon (i.e., a cooked custard with cling to a spoon rather than flowing off), use a small instant-read thermometer to monitor when the custard is ready. If it is heated too much, the custard will curdle, that is, there will be specks of cooked yolk in the mixture. Beating the curdled mixture with another egg yolk will only mask the cooked yolk, not reverse it. It is usually better to start again. Preheating the milk saves a considerable amount of time but is not essential. This makes a sweet, runny custard.

BOILED CUSTARD
makes about 2 cups (500 ml)

2 cups (500 ml) milk
3 egg yolks
¼ cup (50 g) sugar

⅛ teaspoon (0.8 g) salt
½ teaspoon (2.5 ml) vanilla

Bring a saucepan of water to a simmer. In a bowl that will fit over the simmering-water pan, whisk the yolks, sugar, and salt together. Heat the milk in a different saucepan until it is just fizzing around the edges but has not come to a foaming boil. Pour this slowly onto the yolk-sugar mixture, whisking continuously, until well combined. Put this bowl on top of the saucepan of simmering water and whisk continuously until the custard coats a spoon, or has reached about 175°F. Take off the heat and whisk in the vanilla. Set aside to cool.

56 Plum pudding

6 crackers   3 pts milk
¼ cup butter   1 cup sugar   ½ teasp salt
1 teasp mixed spices   6 eggs
1 lb stoned raisins
Soak crackers in milk. Cream butter
& sugar add salt spice & eggs
well beaten & stir mixture into
milk Add raisins. Bake in a deep
pudding dish well buttered with cold
butter for three or four hours over
low flame. Stir several times during
first hour to keep raisins from settling
Serve whipped cream

There are no plums in plum pudding—one largely obsolete meaning of plum was a raisin, only encountered today in combinations like plum pudding or plum cake. We do not know exactly which cracker she used, so we used a fairly neutral Purity cream cracker. For spices, we used a teaspoon of roughly equal quantities of cloves, cinnamon, and nutmeg. The mixture is quite fluid, so when all is mixed together, the cracker crumbs float to the top and the raisins sink to the bottom. As the mixture cooks, it starts to set like a custard, and at that point it needs to be stirred to get the crumbs and the raisins distributed throughout the pudding. When and how often it should be stirred depends on the baking temperature. We translated "low flame" as 250°F oven temperature—erring, if anything, on the low side. At that temperature not much happens for the first hour, but during the second hour of baking the mixture should be stirred until the raisins start to stay afloat at the surface.

This is an uninspiring plum pudding because the egg matrix curdles slightly and weeps liquid; we do not recommend it.

PLUM PUDDING
serves 8 to 10

6 (60 g) crackers
6 cups (1.5 l) milk
¼ cup (55 g) butter, plus extra for greasing
1 cup (200 g) sugar
½ teaspoon (3.3 g) salt
1 teaspoon (3 g) mixed spices
6 eggs
3 cups (450 g) seedless raisins
1 cup (250 ml) cream (optional)

Preheat the oven to 250°F. Grease a 4-quart casserole or equivalent. Crumble the crackers finely (put them in a cloth or plastic bag and pound with a rolling pin or bottle), mix with the milk, and soak for about 15 minutes. Whisk the eggs until homogeneous. Cream the butter and sugar together, then mix in the salt, spices, and eggs. Mix in the cracker crumbs and milk. Stir in the raisins.

Pour the mixture into the prepared casserole, cover, and bake undisturbed for about 1 hour. Then continue baking, but for the next 45 minutes stir the mixture gently every 15 minutes. Then bake for a further 45 minutes undisturbed (i.e., 2½ hours in total), or until the pudding has set completely. If desired, whip the cream to soft peaks, and serve with portions of the plum pudding.

---

57 Blueberry cake or muffins

1 teasp soda   2 teasp cream tartar
1 cup sugar   2 ½ cups flour   ½ cup milk
1 egg   Butter size 1 egg   1 pt. blueberries
Mix and sift dry ingredients
reserving ½ cup flour to mix with
berries work in butter add milk
gradually egg well beaten & blue
berries mixed with reserved flour
Bake over a medium flame

Agnes Ayre's Notebook

A good basic blueberry cake. The only problem with the recipe is that the batter gets impossibly stiff because there is not enough liquid. Increasing the milk, as in the recipe below, works much better.

BLUEBERRY CAKE OR MUFFINS
makes one 8-inch (20 cm) round cake or 12 muffins

1 cup (200 g) sugar
¼ cup (55 g) butter
1 egg
2 cups (300 g) flour
1 teaspoon (5 g) baking soda

2 teaspoons (10 g) cream of tartar
1 cup (250 ml) milk
2 cups (220 g) blueberries
½ cup (75 g) flour

Preheat the oven to 350°F. Grease and flour a 3-inch-deep, 8-inch round cake pan. Cream the butter and sugar together. Beat in the egg. Mix the 2 cups of flour, baking soda, and cream of tartar.

Beat portions of the flour mixture into the butter-sugar mixture, alternating with milk. When thoroughly mixed, toss the blueberries with the ½ cup of flour to coat them. Fold the coated berries and any residual flour into the cake batter. Pour and scrape this mixture into the prepared pan and bake 55 to 60 minutes, or until a small skewer inserted into the thickest part comes out clean. Turn out on a rack to cool.

Evening Telegram, March 28, 1918.

To make muffins, grease and flour 12 standard (3 x 1¼-inch) muffin cups. Divide the batter between the cups, smoothing off the tops with the back of a wetted spoon. Bake 25 to 30 minutes, or until a small skewer inserted into the thickest part comes out clean. Turn out on racks to cool.

58 Baking powder biscuits

2 cups flour   1 teasp salt   4 teasp baking powder - 1 tablesp butter 1 tablesp lard   ¾ cup equal parts milk & water
Mix flour, salt & baking powder & sift twice. Work in butter & lard with finger tips add milk & water gradually - mixing with knife When just stiff enough to be handled turn on a well floured board and toss till well-floured but do not knead the dough
Pat with pin until dough is of ½ inch thickness. Shape with small biscuit cutter. Bake over high flame.

These are unsweetened, savoury biscuits in the American sense, not biscuits as in sweet cookies. Sifting the flour, baking powder, and salt is not necessary if they are mixed thoroughly. Treat the dough gently; as Mrs. Ayre says, do not knead it—act more as if you are making pastry.

BAKING POWDER BISCUITS
makes 16 to 18 biscuits

2 cups (300 g) flour
1 teaspoon (6.5 g) salt
4 teaspoons (20 g) baking powder
1 tablespoon (15 g) butter
1 tablespoon (15 g) lard
¾ cup (190 ml) equal parts milk and water

Preheat the oven to 400°F. Lightly grease one or more baking sheets (or use parchment paper or silicone baking mats). Mix the flour, baking powder, and salt. Rub in the lard and butter until both are absorbed by the flour. Gradually add the milk and water in small portions, stirring with a fork (or a knife, as Mrs. Ayre suggests), and press it gently together to make a dough. Turn out onto a floured surface, fold the dough in half, and press down lightly. Repeat 2 or 3 times to make a homogeneous dough. Press or gently roll the dough out to about ½ inch thickness, which will be an approximately 10-inch circle. Cut out disks with a 2¼-inch circular cutter. Gently press and fold the scraps of dough together, roll out again, and cut more disks. Lay the disks on the prepared baking sheet(s) and bake 20 minutes, or until the biscuits are puffed and lightly browned on top. Turn out on a rack to cool.

59 Cream Celery soup.

1 ½ pts milk
1 qt celery cut in pieces   2 tablesp flour
2 tablesp butter   1 slice onion   1 blade mace   1 cup cream. Boil celery in a quart of water 45 minutes. Boil mace, onion & milk together. Mash celery in the water & add to boiling milk. Melt butter in saucepan add flour slowly until it thickens cook 3 or 4 mins & add to boiling soup season. Strain and serve immediately adding 1 cup whipped cream after soup is in tureen.

Both blades of mace and ground mace can be difficult to find, so ground nutmeg can be substituted.

Mrs. Ayre's method is unnecessarily complicated, so while achieving the same result, we have simplified it. The finishing cup of cream is not necessary—but that is a matter of taste.

This soup is at its best when made with fresh, vibrantly green, local celery in the fall. At other times of the year, if using anaemic imported celery, this is thin and tasteless.

CREAM CELERY SOUP
makes 7 to 8 cups (1.7 to 2 l)

4 cups (500 g) celery pieces (about 10–12 stalks)
1 small (50 g, trimmed weight) onion
4 cups (1 l) water
2 tablespoons (20 g) flour
2 tablespoons (30 g) butter
3 cups milk (750 ml)
1½ teaspoons (10 g) salt
½ teaspoon (1.5 g) pepper
1 blade mace, or ¼ teaspoon (0.75 g) nutmeg
1 cup (250 ml) cream (optional)

Cut each celery stalk in half lengthways, and then crossways into ½-inch chunks. Peel and chop the onion. Bring the celery and onion to a boil in the water, and simmer about 45 minutes. In a separate saucepan melt the butter and whisk in the flour. Add the milk, nutmeg, salt, and pepper and bring to a boil, whisking frequently, and simmer about 5 minutes. Reserve off the heat.

Mash the cooked celery and onion into the cooking water. This can be done by hand with, for example, a potato masher, but a hand blender works well. Whisk the mashed celery and onion into the thickened milk mixture, bring back to a boil, and simmer about 5 minutes.

Strain through a sieve, pressing down on the fibrous material to extract all the liquid. Taste and adjust the seasoning. Add part or all of the cream to taste.

60 Welsh rarebit

¼ lb cheese   ¼ cup milk
1 egg   1 teasp salt   1 teasp mustard
1 tablesp butter   pinch cayenne.
Melt cheese in saucepan mix melted
butter salt mustard & cayenne with a
 little cold milk & add to cheese then
add egg, beaten slightly & last of all
milk serve on toast or crackers low flame

Mrs. Ayre originally wrote Welsh rabbit, but then wrote rarebit over the top. *Rabbit* is in fact the older term; *rarebit* came later and was likely adopted as a seemingly more genteel name. Mrs. Ayre seems caught between the two.

Cheese quality is all-important here. It has to be a hard cheese, something with personality, such as a sharp, aged cheddar. Using the full 1 teaspoon of salt is excessive because there is plenty of salt in the cheese; we recommend using only ¼ teaspoon—at most ½ teaspoon if you like food on the salty side.

Her method is unnecessarily complicated and melting the cheese first risks scorching it. We recommend the procedure outlined below. This makes a good basic Welsh Rabbit, if the salt is reduced.

WELSH RABBIT/RAREBIT
serves 4

1½ cups (112 g) cheese
¼ cup (65 ml) milk
1 egg
¼ teaspoon (1.5 g) salt
1 teaspoon (5 g) dry mustard

1 tablespoon (15 g) butter
1 pinch (0.1 g) cayenne
4 slices bread
butter for the toast

Toast 4 slices of bread, butter them, and keep warm (or do this at the last minute). Put the butter, salt, mustard, cayenne, and milk in a small saucepan and heat gently. Whisk to break up any lumps in the dry mustard. When it is warm and the butter completely melted, grate the cheese into it and continue to heat gently until the cheese is just melted, whisking occasionally. Break the egg directly into the cheese mixture and whisk briskly to make a homogeneous mixture. Continue to heat and whisk until the mixture thickens slightly, and you notice one or two large bubbles popping at the surface. Divide the mixture between the buttered toast and serve at once.

61 Scalloped eggs with fish, sausage, chicken etc

6 hard boiled eggs   ¾ cup chopped meat or fish.   ¾ cup buttered cracker crumbs   1 pt white sauce

Sprinkle the bottom of buttered dish with crumbs cover with ½ the eggs chopped finely. Cover eggs with sauce & sauce with meat - then repeat & cover top with crumbs Bake over medium flame until crumbs brown.

This is another way of frugally using minimal leftovers to make another meal. The ¾ cup of fish, sausage, or chicken is only about 5 ounces—about one single chicken breast, which can be stretched generously for 4 people.

If you don't have a favourite way of hard-boiling eggs: put the eggs straight from the refrigerator into a small saucepan with just enough water to cover. Bring to a boil and simmer 10 minutes. Immediately transfer the eggs to a bowl of excess cold water.

When the eggs are cool, peel and chop them. Although Mrs. Ayre says to chop the eggs finely, this dish works best if some texture is left, so chop them only to about the size of a whole, dry pea.

An easy way to reduce the crackers to crumbs is put them in a cloth or plastic bag and pound with a rolling pin (or wine bottle) until nothing bigger than a split pea remains.

The white sauce she mentions is béchamel, and making it is described below.

The instructions about layering the ingredients are ambiguous, but are not critical as long as a layer of crumbs sits atop a layer of sauce.

This makes a very tasty, savoury lunch or light supper for four people, or can be stretched further with bread and butter and a salad on the side.

SCALLOPED EGGS WITH FISH, SAUSAGE, CHICKEN, etc.
serves 4

¾ cup (75 g) cracker crumbs
1 tablespoon (15 g) butter,
    plus extra to grease the dish
6 hard-boiled eggs

¾ cup (150 g) chopped fish, sausage, or chicken
2 cups (500 ml) béchamel sauce

For the béchamel sauce

4 tablespoons (60 g) butter
4 tablespoons (40 g) flour
½ teaspoon (3.3 g) salt
¼ teaspoon (0.75 g) black pepper
¼ teaspoon (0.75 g) nutmeg
2 cups (500 ml) milk

Preheat the oven to 350°F. Hard-boil the eggs, peel, and chop them. Break the crackers into crumbs, melt the butter, and toss with the crumbs. Chop the cooked chicken (or whatever you are using) into ¼-inch dice.

For the white sauce: melt the butter, whisk in the flour until smooth, then whisk in the milk and heat gently until it thickens and starts to boil. Reduce the heat, whisk in the salt, nutmeg, and pepper, and simmer about 5 minutes, whisking occasionally.

Butter an 8 by 8-inch or equivalent size baking dish, spread half the buttered crumbs evenly on the bottom, then half the chopped eggs, half the sauce, all the diced chicken, half the chopped eggs, half the sauce, and half the buttered crumbs on top. Bake about 60 minutes, or until the crumbs are lightly browned and the sauce bubbles up at the sides. Serve hot.

> ## 62 Ham Souffle
>
> 2 cups minced ham
> add white egg & beat until smooth
> add dash paprika   1 cup whipped
> cream & whites 2 eggs beaten stiff
> Pour into oiled mould   Bake over
> low flame & serve hot with tomato sauce

Mrs. Ayre would have chopped the ham by hand, or perhaps put it through a meat grinder. A food processor does the job efficiently and quickly, but do not reduce the ham to a mush: pulse a few times until some texture is still left.

Grease the mould with butter as oil tends to bead on the surface and the soufflé will stick in places.

Whip the single egg white before mixing with the ham to ensure complete and thorough mixing.

The dash of paprika does not add much flavour, but as it offsets the paleness of the mixture, we increased the amount.

But after all the trouble of making it, this recipe does not work. The soufflé ends up as a watery mess rather than a puffed glory because the cream and the egg whites break down and ooze fluid. To make the recipe work would be more like radical surgery rather than simple tweaking. If Mrs. Ayre's cook ever served this to the family, she would tactfully have used an entirely different recipe based on the same amount of ham.

HAM SOUFFLÉ
supposed to serve 4

2 cups (250 g) minced ham
1 egg white
¼ teaspoon (0.75 g) paprika

1 cup (250 ml) cream
2 egg whites

Preheat the oven to 350°F. Lightly grease a 2-quart mould. Chop the ham finely by hand or pulse a few times in a food processor. Whip the 1 egg white to soft peaks and then mix thoroughly with the minced ham and paprika.

Whip the cream to stiff peaks and fold it into the ham mixture. Beat the 2 egg whites to stiff peaks and fold these in. Pour and scrape this into the greased mould and bake for about 30 to 35 minutes, or until the soufflé is browned on top.

63 Cream dressing.

1 tablesp butter
¼ teasp salt,   2 tablesp sugar
2 tablesp vinegar 2 eggs ½ pt cream
Beat eggs add sugar salt vinegar
& butter cook in double boiler
until thickens cool & add the cream
whipped

This is the second recipe for cream dressing (see recipe 42). They differ in both taste and texture but are similar in that both are finished with whipped cream, and both would have been used for similar purposes.

Make sure that the water in the double boiler is barely simmering, because the eggs thicken quickly with so little added liquid. Whisk more or less continuously, scraping the bowl with the side of the whisk to make sure that the egg does not set at the edges.

This dressing resembles a rather bland, creamy mayonnaise. It is too thick to use on a green salad, but works well on something like potato salad, where the cubes of potato can be turned vigorously in the dressing to coat them.

CREAM DRESSING
makes about 1½ cups (375 ml)

2 eggs
2 tablespoons (25 g) sugar
2 tablespoons (30 ml) vinegar
¼ teaspoon (1.5 g) salt
1 tablespoon (15 g) butter
1 cup (250 ml) cream

Beat the eggs until pale yellow, then beat in the sugar, salt, and vinegar. Add the butter, then heat gently in a double boiler. Whisk continually until the butter melts and the mixture thickens. Set aside to cool. When cool, whip the cream to soft peaks and fold it in.

64 Apple or Berry Roll

Make biscuit dough place on top 4 or 5 sour apples chopped finely Roll & place in casserole or buttered pan. Make a syrup by boiling together for 5 mins 1 cup sugar ½ cup water ½ teasp cinnamon or nutmeg. Pour half over roll saving remainder to serve as sauce. Bake ½ hour in an uncovered pan basting with syrup. ~~With berries add 1 cup milk & 1 cup blue, black or raspberries, which have been rolled in flour.~~

The last three lines have been crossed out because she clearly decided to create a separate recipe for the berry pudding that comes next.

Biscuit doughs are essentially savoury, baking-powder doughs from the American tradition and are much like Newfoundland tea buns or English scones but with no sugar or eggs. There is no recipe described here, so the biscuit dough in recipe 58 can be used.

Four or 5 apples are listed in the recipe, but that many apples would need at least double the amount of biscuit dough, which would yield an enormous apple roll, enough to feed more than a dozen. We recommend a single batch of dough with only 2 apples.

As the boiling sugar and cinnamon is prone to boiling over, use a low heat, just enough to keep it boiling gently.

APPLE ROLL
serves 6

- 1 recipe biscuit dough, recipe 58 or similar
- 2 sour apples (400 g, total unpeeled weight), Granny Smith or any tart apple
- 1 cup (200 g) sugar
- ½ cup (125 ml) water
- ½ teaspoon (1.5 g) cinnamon or nutmeg

Preheat the oven to 350°F. Lightly grease an 8 by 10-inch baking pan (or use parchment paper or a silicone mat). Make the biscuit dough and roll it out on a lightly floured surface to a rectangle about 8 by 16 inches. Peel, core, and chop the apples into about ½-inch pieces. Spread the diced apple over the dough, leaving 1 inch uncovered on each side, then roll it up and place it seam-down on the greased pan.

Boil the sugar, water, and cinnamon or nutmeg for 5 minutes. Pour about half over the apple roll, reserving the other half. Bake the roll for 50 to 60 minutes, uncovered, until a small skewer inserted through the centre meets no resistance from the apple and comes out clean. Baste the roll with the syrup in the pan (not the reserved portion) about every 10 minutes for the first half hour; after that, the syrup will have dried up, making basting impossible. Serve warm, with the reserved sugar-cinnamon/nutmeg sauce drizzled on top of each portion.

65 Berry Pudding.

*Make biscuit dough
add 1 cup milk & 1 cup blueberries
raspberries or blackberries which
have been rolled in flour. Put
in buttered mould (a five lb lard pail
may be used) steam 1 hour.)*

A 5-pound lard pail holds about 2½ quarts, so any mould of the same or slightly larger capacity is good. A 3-quart pudding basin allows plenty of room for expansion.

For this recipe, use a total of 1¾ cups of milk when making the basic biscuit dough (the original ¾ cup plus 1 cup extra).

This recipe needs sugar. It may have been left out of the recipe, or a sweet sauce to accompany it may have been intended. If the former, add about ¼ cup of sugar to the biscuit dough; if the latter, try a simple sauce of warm molasses with a shot of rum. We liked this with both sugar in the dough *and* molasses sauce poured on each portion.

BERRY PUDDING
serves 4 to 6

1 recipe biscuit dough (58 or similar) with an extra 1 cup (250 ml) milk and ¼ cup (50 g) sugar added to the dough

1 cup (120 g) blueberries, raspberries, or blackberries
1 tablespoon (10 g) flour
butter to grease the pudding basin

For the sauce (optional)
1 cup molasses   3 tablespoons (45 ml) dark rum

Butter a 3-quart pudding basin or any mould of similar capacity. Make a biscuit dough. Roll the berries in 1 tablespoon of flour, shake off the surplus in a sieve, then mix the floured berries into the dough. Scrape into the buttered pudding basin, tie a cotton cloth over the top, and place in a steamer. Steam for 1 hour. Do not let the steamer boil dry; check the water level about halfway through and add boiling water as necessary.

If serving with the sauce, warm the molasses, mix in the rum, and pour a couple of tablespoons over each portion.

Sugar is Scarce

AND HIGH IN PRICE.

Why not buy and use "good, honest" MOLASSES instead?

We offer to-day at lowest prices a small shipment of

Choice Barbados Grocery Molasses,

in Tierces and Barrels.

Tierces average about 34 gallons each and Barrels average about 22 gallons each. Let us have your order for a Tierce or Barrel or more while this consignment remains unsold.

F. McNAMARA,

QUEEN STREET.

tu,th,s

Evening Telegram, December 3, 1918.

66 Paste

1 ½ cups flour   ½ cup lard
or lard and butter in equal parts
½ teasp salt. Cold water.
Mix flour & salt. Reserve 1¼
tablesp lard & work remainder into
flour using a knife. With cold water
moisten to a dough. Toss on a
floured board pat & roll out. Spread
with 1 tablesp lard dredge with
flour, roll, pat and roll out. Roll
up again & cut from end of roll
a piece large enough to line a pie
plate Roll this piece out keeping it
as nearly circular as possible
Use the remainder of the lard or lard
and butter to dot over the top crust
of pie before putting it in the oven to
give the pie a flaky appearance.
This amount of paste will make two
pies with one crust or one pie with
two crusts. & a few puffs

It is interesting that Mrs. Ayre was still using the Middle English word *paste*, which shares an origin in Late Latin with the French *pâte*. That French word is still alive and well, but the English word gradually fell out of use during the first half of the 20th century as the alternative word *pastry* gained prominence.

The fats can be cut in with repeated chops of a small knife, as she recommends, or more conveniently with a multi-bladed pastry cutter. Add as little extra water as possible. This makes a thin pastry when rolled to fit a 9-inch pie plate, so be careful when handling it after rolling out.

Mrs. Ayre's technique of spreading the partly rolled dough with a skim of fat and then rerolling is an attempt to imitate the multilayered nature of puff pastry. This does not work—the resulting cooked pastry is no different from that produced by cutting in all the fat at the start, which we recommend. However, if you want to attempt Mrs. Ayre's method, we have tried to explicate her rather confusing instructions in the method below.

PASTE
makes pastry for 1 double-crust pie or 2 single crusts

- 1½ cups (225 g) flour
- ½ teaspoon (3.3 g) salt
- ½ cup (100 g) lard, or ¼ cup (50 g) lard plus ¼ cup (50 g) butter
- 5 tablespoons (75 ml) cold water, plus extra if needed
- 1 teaspoon (3 g) extra flour for sprinkling on the dough

Mix the 1½ cups of flour with the salt. Reserve about 1¼ tablespoons of the lard. Cut the bulk of the lard into the flour and salt. Make a well in the centre of the mixture, pour in the cold water, and stir until the dough just holds together. If the dough fails to hold together, stir in more water, about ½ teaspoon at a time until it does.

Turn the dough out onto a lightly floured surface, press into a rough rectangle, then roll it out to about 8 by 10 inches. Spread with 1 tablespoon of reserved lard, sprinkle evenly with 1 teaspoon of flour, roll it up by hand into a cylinder, press it out into a rough rectangle, and roll out again to about 8 by 10 inches. Roll by hand into a roughly 10-inch cylinder and cut in half into two short cylinders.

Roll one cylinder into a circle. The other cylinder will become either the pastry for another single-crust pie or the top layer of a double-crust pie. Any remaining scraps of pastry can be re-rolled and a few decorative shapes of pastry cut from it for garnishes.

The remaining ¼ tablespoon of lard is reserved and dotted on top of the finished pie (see recipe 67).

67 Apple Pie.

4 or 5 sour apples ⅓ cup sugar
¼ teasp grated nutmeg or cinnamon
⅛ teasp salt 1 teasp butter 1 teasp lemon juice. Pare & cut apples then slices
Line a pie plate with paste. Put a row of slices of apple around the plate ½ inch from edge & work toward centre until plate is covered then pile on the rest. Mix sugar spice salt & lemon juice & sprinkle over apple then put butter in small pieces over the top. Wet edges & press together. Cut a few holes for steam. Bake 45 use low flame.

Tart apples such as Granny Smiths work best here because they retain some texture and the whole pie does not get overly sweet. Layer the apple slices into the pie, occasionally chopping a few slices into small dice and filling the spaces between the slices—do this as often as necessary to pack all the apple into the pie. Cinnamon gives a better flavour than nutmeg but do not be tempted to add more, ¼ teaspoon is enough. This makes a good, basic apple pie.

APPLE PIE
makes 1 double-crust 9-inch (23 cm) pie

1 recipe of pastry (66)
4 or 5 (about 800 g, total unpeeled weight) tart apples, e.g., Granny Smith
⅓ cup (70 g) sugar
¼ teaspoon (0.75 g) cinnamon or nutmeg
⅛ teaspoon (0.8 g) salt
1 teaspoon (5 ml) lemon juice
1 teaspoon (5 g) butter

Preheat the oven to 350°F. Roll out half the pastry on a lightly floured surface to about an 11-inch circle and line a 9-inch pie plate, making sure the rim is covered. Slice the trimmed apple pieces thinly. Spread slices carefully over the layer of pastry (but not over the rim) to make sure that the pastry is completely covered, then add the rest of the slices more haphazardly.

Mix the sugar, salt, and cinnamon and sprinkle the mixture evenly over the apples, then sprinkle with the lemon juice. Dot with split-pea-sized pieces of butter. Roll out the other portion of pastry to the same size, wet the rim of the pastry in the plate, lay the second layer of pastry over the apple slices, and press the rims of the pastry together. Squeeze the two layers firmly together with a series of thumbprints, or crimp with a fork for a more decorative edge. Cut a cross in the top to allow steam to escape. Bake 50 to 60 minutes, or until the pastry is lightly browned and the juices start to bubble through in places. Serve warm or cold.

68 (a) Blueberry Pie.

*Same. Dredge berries with flour
Rhubarb & Strawberry. Cut fine and put in oven
to dry. Cover paste level add 1 cup sugar
little butter & salt & layer strawberries.*

Two recipes here, but both are extensions of 67. The floured berries thicken the juice rather than prevent them from sinking into the batter.

BLUEBERRY PIE
makes one 9-inch (23 cm) pie

1 recipe of pastry (66)
3 cups (350 g) blueberries
2 tablespoons (20 g) flour
⅓ cup (70 g) sugar
⅛ teaspoon (0.8 g) salt
¼ teaspoon (0.75 g) cinnamon
1 teaspoon (5 ml) lemon juice
1 teaspoon (5 g) butter

Preheat the oven to 350°F. Make the pastry. Line a 9-inch pie plate. Roll the berries in the flour, then spread them evenly over the pastry. Mix the sugar, salt, and cinnamon and sprinkle evenly over the blueberries. Sprinkle with lemon juice. Dot with split-pea-sized pieces of butter. Cover with pastry and proceed as in recipe 67.

Because rhubarb is full of water, getting rid of some of the liquid before putting it in a pie is a useful trick. The method is described below.

RHUBARB & STRAWBERRY PIE
makes one 9-inch (23 cm) pie

1 recipe of pastry (66)
2 cups (225 g) rhubarb
1 cup (200 g) sugar
⅛ teaspoon (0.8 g) salt
1 tablespoon (15 g) butter
2 cups (250 g) strawberries

Preheat the oven to 350°F. Slice the rhubarb ½ inch thick. Spread it out on a baking sheet and dry out in the oven until the surplus liquid has evaporated. Cool. Slice the strawberries. Line a 9-inch pie plate with pastry and spread the cooled rhubarb evenly over the top. Sprinkle the sugar and salt over the rhubarb, dot with split-pea-sized pieces of butter, then spread the sliced strawberries over the top. Cover with pastry, then proceed as in recipe 67.

68 (b) Cup Custard.

4 cups hot milk
4 eggs   ½ cup sugar   ¼ teasp salt
nutmeg.
Beat eggs slightly add sugar & salt
then pour on slowly hot milk
Strain mixture into cups, place cups
in a pan of hot water & sprinkle
a few gratings of nutmeg over each
one. Bake over a low flame until
firm & a knife can b inserted
& removed without custard sticking
to it. Do not let water in pan
boil or custard will whey.

This is a set rather than a pouring custard (recipe 55). Preheating the milk not only speeds up the process but makes it possible to standardize the timing—if it is preheated to the same temperature each time, you will know how long to bake a custard next time. Preheat the milk in a small saucepan on top of the stove but do not boil to the point of foaming up; scald only until it fizzes around the edges. Microwaving the milk also works well: heat to about 203°F.

Mrs. Ayre recommends straining the mixture, which is not strictly necessary but is useful to remove any bits of milk-skin if the milk has been slightly overheated and remove the chalazae, which can be substantial in fresh eggs and end up as little white coils in the finished custard.

The ⅛ teaspoon of nutmeg is only a guide. The problem with pre-grating the nutmeg is that if it is pinched between thumb and forefinger to sprinkle on the tops, it clumps together and falls in a lump on the top of the custard, rather than being dispersed across the top. It is better and easier to grate the nutmeg directly onto the custards before putting them in the oven, and judge the amount by eye.

Mrs. Ayre used cups to bake this custard; we used large ramekins (each about a 10-ounce capacity). For a water bath, select a wide, shallow saucepan or baking pan that will hold the ramekins with a little space between them. A 13-inch-diameter, 4-inch-deep pan was used in testing this recipe. Have a kettle of freshly boiled water ready; the above pan will need about 2 quarts of boiling water. After the filled ramekins are in the pan, very carefully pour the boiling water into the pan, taking care not to splash into the ramekins. If the ramekins are a tight fit, remove one to create a space where the boiling water can be poured, then replace it before putting the pan in the oven. The water should come about one-half to three-quarters way up the ramekins.

The setting point is problematic in this recipe because there is proportionately less egg to the volume of milk than in a standard baked custard, which makes for a soft and fragile custard, difficult to estimate when it is cooked. Mrs. Ayre recommends the sticking-a-knife-in technique, which is fine, but the difference between an undercooked and a cooked soft custard is tricky. Another technique is to reach into the oven and nudge the side of the pan, and see if the custard sloshes (not cooked) or just wobbles (cooked); again, with such a soft custard it is a tricky distinction. The times given below work for the size of ramekin and temperatures we used. But they are forgiving, so if in doubt, give them an extra 5 minutes in the oven.

CUP CUSTARD
serves 6

4 cups (1 l) hot milk
4 eggs
½ cup (100 g) sugar
¼ teaspoon (1.5 g) salt
⅛ teaspoon (0.4 g) nutmeg

Preheat the oven to 350°F. Beat the eggs with the salt and sugar until homogeneous. Scald the milk (or heat in a microwave to about 180°F), whisk it into the eggs and sugar, then strain this mixture into a separate bowl. Divide equally between 6 large ramekins.

Boil a kettle of water. Grate nutmeg over the tops of the the custards, and place them in a wide saucepan or baking pan that just holds the ramekins comfortably. Carefully pour the boiling water into the pan, until at least halfway up the ramekins.

Slide the pan into the oven. Bake for about 45 to 55 minutes, or until the custard only wobbles when the edge of the pan is nudged, or until a small, thin knife inserted into the custard comes out clean. Remove the ramekins from the water bath, cool, then refrigerate until ready to serve.

69 Prunes

*Cover bottom of a buttered
dish with coarse bread crumbs
Cover with cooked prunes (minus seeds)
dust with sugar cinnamon & nutmeg
Pour over ⅓ cup milk repeat &
cover top with buttered crumbs.
Bake till brown*

Mrs. Ayre is particularly economical with her instructions for this recipe. Trial and error resulted in the recipe below, and it is surprisingly good, given the rather unpromising ingredients. Use only fresh bread crumbs—do not be tempted to use dry bread crumbs, which will end up a soggy mess. This is really a square, and can be cut into small portions when cooled. But it is perhaps best served warm, with a thin custard (see recipe 55) poured over each serving.

PRUNES
serves 4 to 6

1 quart (650 g) pitted prunes
2 cups (500 ml) water
2½ cups (200 g) fresh bread crumbs
2 tablespoons (30 g) butter,
   plus extra to grease the dish

¼ cup (50 g) sugar
¼ teaspoon (0.75 g) cinnamon
⅓ cup (80 ml) milk

Preheat the oven to 350°F. Butter an 8 by 8-inch baking dish. Put the prunes in a medium saucepan with the water. Add extra water as necessary to barely cover the prunes. Bring to a boil and simmer about 15 minutes. Pour into a sieve and let drain.

Spread about 1 cup of bread crumbs in the buttered baking dish. Carefully place half the cooked prunes on top of the crumbs, taking care not to mix up them up. Mix the sugar and cinnamon, then sprinkle this evenly over the prunes. Distribute the other half of the cooked prunes on top, and pour in the milk.

Melt the butter and toss with the remaining 1½ cups of crumbs, tossing them as you do so. Spread the buttered crumbs over the prunes. Bake about 30 minutes, or until the crumbs are lightly browned.

70 Hermits

> 2 cups brown sugar 1 cup butter
> 3 eggs, 1 teasp soda flour to mix a soft dough   2 tablesp hot water, 1 cup chopped raisins ⅛ teasp ginger 1 sm teasp each of cinnamon cloves & nutmeg
> Combine brown sugar, butter & yolks of eggs well beaten add whites of eggs beaten until stiff, soda dissolved in hot water two cups of flour mixed and sifted with spices and raisins mixed with a little flour, then add enough more flour to mix to a soft dough
> Roll out shape and make as molasses cookies. Use high flame.

Whipping the egg whites adds no leavening to the finished dough, because all the air gets kneaded out, but it does help the egg whites mix easily with the sugar and butter. The 2 cups (300 g) of flour to make the dough underestimates the total amount needed. In addition to the 2 cups specified, almost as much again is necessary; the recipe below is a little more realistic about the amount of flour needed.

The raisins do not have to be chopped finely, just make sure there are no (or few) whole ones left. The instruction to mix the chopped raisins with a little flour is unnecessary; mix the chopped raisins into the flour-spice mixture, breaking up any clumps.

HERMITS
makes about 48

2 cups (300 g) brown sugar
1 cup (220 g) butter
3 eggs
1 teaspoon (5 g) baking soda
2 tablespoons (30 ml) warm water
1 cup (150 g) raisins

3 cups flour (450 g), plus about an extra 1 cup (150 g) or more
⅛ teaspoon (0.4 g) ginger
½ teaspoon (1.5 g) cinnamon
½ teaspoon (1.5 g) cloves
½ teaspoon (1.5 g) nutmeg

Preheat the oven to 400°F. Lightly grease 3 or 4 baking sheets, or use parchment paper or silicone baking mats. Separate the eggs. Chop the raisins. Beat the brown sugar, butter, and egg yolks together. Dissolve the baking soda in the warm water and mix in. Beat the egg whites stiff and fold these into the mixture. Mix in the chopped raisins and spices. Mix in the 3 cups of flour, then turn the dough out onto a floured surface and knead in more flour. Continue kneading, sprinkling with extra flour, until the dough barely sticks to your fingers.

For convenience, divide the dough into halves. Roll out one to a 12-inch circle, which will be about ¼ inch thick. Cut about 18 circles, each 2½ inches in diameter, plus another 6 from the re-rolled scraps. Carefully lift the disks with a thin spatula. If the dough is too soft and sticks to the surface and crumples when the spatula is slid underneath it, gather it up and knead in another ¼ cup of flour, then roll out again. Roll out the other half of the dough, and cut a total of about 48 disks. Lay on several prepared baking sheets, and bake 12 to 14 minutes, or until the tops are well browned.

Spices, Pepper, Ginger,
in 6-lb. Boxes, Pure and Compound.

BOWRING BROTHERS, Limited,
332   GROCERY, St. John's.   332.
.m,w,f,tf

Evening Telegram, October 2, 1918.

71 Canning.

Always use a porcelain-lined or granite ware kettle. Fruit for canning should be fresh, perfect & not over-ripe Allow one-third its weight in sugar and two & ½ or 3 cups water to each pound of sugar. Make a thin sirup by boiling sugar & water ten minutes [? obscured] [cook?] a small quantity [obscured] fruit at a time in the sirup & the fruit may keep its shape. When filling the jars if there is not enough sirup add boiling water as the jars must be filled to over-flowing. Heat the jars gradually by rolling them in water. Then set them in a pan of warm water & pour boiling water into them. Turn out water place rubbers which have been dipped in hot water & fill immediately letting the jars stand in the pan of water or on a cloth wrung from hot water while being filled. Insert a spoon between fruit and jar that air bubbles may rise to the top. Place covers which have been standing in hot water & fasten tightly. Use new rubbers each season. Parawax when cool dip tops in melted wax.

These are general notes on canning, which here means bottling (putting things in glass jars with a sealable lid). Originally such jars had separate rubber gaskets under reusable glass lids, whereas now—at least in North America—the disposable metal lid has an integral gasket. Both old and new lids are held in place by threaded rings.

Graniteware, a type of enamelware with an applied pattern which was popular in Newfoundland from the end of the 19th century through the interwar years, was relatively cheap and impervious to cooking acids, so it was often used to hold acidic foods.

Some of Mrs. Ayre's general instructions are still valid and useful, especially about selecting fruit that is ripe but not overripe for bottling. And where a syrup is called for, her recipe is still generally applicable. Inserting a long spoon handle into a jar to help air bubbles rise to the surface is a good idea, and using new rubbers (i.e., gaskets between lid and jar) is sound advice—simply use new lids each time.

But, in general, it is never wise to rely on pre-World War II bottling instructions. At best they are unnecessarily elaborate, as in Mrs. Ayre's notebook, and seem designed to sterilize the jars, rings, and caps without the need for processing in a boiling water bath afterwards. Or they are of marginal value, like dipping the tops of the filled jars in melted wax. This was intended to create a back-up seal in case the rubber gasket failed or was not properly sealed in the first place. The modern gasket as part of the lid is foolproof once a proper seal has been achieved. Some old instructions are plain wrong, like her injunction to fill the jars to overflowing; jars should not be completely full, a headspace of at least ½ inch of air must be left.

As a general guide, always use modern methods for old bottling recipes. Because the purpose of this book is to comment on Mrs. Ayre's recipes, rather than be a reference for modern techniques, in general we only outline the modern process that should be adopted for her recipes. For example, we frequently direct cooks to put on lids and threaded rings and process in a boiling water bath. This is already familiar to many cooks, but if in doubt consult any standard work on preserving for details. In particular, *and most importantly*, bottling non-acidic foods like fish or meat should only be attempted if you have both the knowledge and specialized equipment, due to a risk of potentially fatal botulism poisoning. The old advice to boil such jars of foods for 3 hours (e.g., see recipe 135) does *not* guarantee safety.

72 Canned Raspberries or strawberries

Select firm raspberries or firm rather small strawberries Heat jars & fill them to the rim with berries Make a sirup of equal parts sugar & water Pour boiling sirup over fruit filling the jars to over-flowing & snap the covers. Place jars in a tub or other receptacle deep enough to hold water to cover them. Pour boiling water into the tub until jars are submerged & allow them to stand in the water until it is cold when fruit will be found perfectly cooked. Berries

See the general notes about bottling in recipe 71. As indicated, do not use whole, large strawberries—they leave too much wasted space between them in the jar. Ideally, use strawberries about the size of raspberries, or cut up larger ones. It is a good idea to buy berries in season, when they are at their peak, bottle all the small ones, and use the rest for other purposes. Particularly with raspberries, because a lot of air can be trapped in the jar, use her trick of inserting the handle of a small spoon into the jar and jostling the berries around to release any air.

CANNED RASPBERRIES OR STRAWBERRIES
fills three 2-cup (500 ml) Mason jars

2 quarts (900 g) raspberries   1 cup (250 ml) water
1 cup (200 g) sugar

Bring the sugar and water to a boil and simmer for 5 minutes to make a syrup. Pack the raspberries into Mason jars. Add about ½ cup of the syrup to each jar. Put on the lids and threaded rings and process in a boiling water bath.

> *73 Blueberries*
>
> *Pick over berries, wash them & place in a preserving kettle with just enough water to keep them from burning. Cook until soft & put in jars.*

See the general notes about bottling in recipe 71. The preliminary cooking releases the juice, which substitutes for a syrup, thereby concentrating the flavour. Cook the berries on a very gentle heat to release the juice without any scorching.

Depending on the size and juiciness of the berries and how much evaporation has occurred during the heating, there may be slightly more simmered berries and juice than are needed to fill the 4 jars to capacity. Leave some clear headspace; do *not* fill the bottles too full.

BLUEBERRIES (bottled)
fills four 2-cup (500 ml) Mason jars

4 quarts (2 kg) blueberries   4 tablespoons (60 ml) water

Put the blueberries in a saucepan, add the water, and place on a very low heat. The mixture does not have to actually boil; bring it to the point where the berries are sitting more or less covered by their own juice and looking a bit wrinkled. Transfer them to Mason jars. Put on the lids and threaded rings and process in a boiling water bath.

74 Strawberry Short-Cake

¾ cup corn meal
1 ¾ cups flour   1 teasp salt   4 teasp
Baking powder   2 tablesp sugar
2 table sortening   ¾ cup cold milk
½ cup cream (whipped)
3 cups strawberries
Sift dry ingredients into a bowl
Add shortening & rub in very lightly
Add milk slowly, mixing with
fork or knife. Turn the dough
out on floured board & roll lightly
one inch thick   Brush top with
milk and bake in hot oven 20 to
25 mins. Split open and spread between
layers with strawberries which
have been sweetened and crushed
Put on top layer. Spread with
whipped cream slightly sweetened
& place berries on top and serve
Raspberries, peaches or bananas instead.

Rather than baking this cake free-form, it can be pressed into a greased and floured 8-inch round cake pan.

STRAWBERRY SHORTCAKE
makes one 8-inch (20 cm) cake

¾ cup (120 g) cornmeal
1¾ cups (265 g) flour
4 teaspoons (20 g) baking powder
2 tablespoons (25 g) sugar
1 teaspoon (6.5 g) salt
2 tablespoons (30 g) shortening or butter

¾ cup (190 ml) cold milk
3 cups (375 g) whole strawberries
sugar as needed to sweeten the strawberries
½ cup (125 ml) cream
1 tablespoon (12.5 g) sugar

Preheat the oven to 400°F. Lightly grease a baking sheet, or use parchment paper or a silicone mat. Or if preferred, grease and flour an 8-inch cake pan.

Mix the cornmeal, flour, baking powder, salt, and the 2 tablespoons of sugar. Rub in the shortening or butter until no lumps can be felt. Mix in the milk, turn out on a lightly floured surface, and press the dough together into a fat disk. Roll out (or pat with your hands) to a 1-inch-thick disk about 7 inches in diameter. Press the edges in with your hand to keep it approximately circular. Pick the disk up with two wide spatulas and place on the prepared baking sheet (or press the dough into the prepared cake pan). Bake about 25 minutes, or until a small skewer inserted in the thickest part comes out clean. Leave on the baking sheet to cool, or turn out from the pan onto a rack.

Mash about half the strawberries. If they are perfectly ripe, they will mash easily, and will need little or no extra sweetening. Otherwise, chop them finely by hand or purée in a food processor, and add as much sugar as needed.

When the cake is cool, split it in half horizontally. Spread the bottom half with the mashed or puréed strawberries, and cap with the top half. Whip the cream with the 1 tablespoon of sugar to stiff peaks, and spread evenly over the top of the cake. Cut all the remaining strawberries in half, or slice large ones, and arrange on top of the cake, pushing them into the cream layer.

75 Bath buns

½ lb flour (spare)
1 tablesp rice flour   1 oz minced peel   2 oz lard   ½ gill milk
1 egg (small) pinch salt. 2 oz white sugar 2 teasp baking powder (level)
Sift flour salt powder add peel
melt lard add sugar & milk to it
& stir into flour - pour in beaten
egg & a few drops essence & mix
well together & place in rough
heaps in a greased tin & put in a
quick oven 5 minutes and reduce heat
for 15 longer to finish cooking

Named for the city in the west of England, Bath buns, first recorded in the 18th century, were originally made from a yeast-leavened, brioche-style dough with candied seeds. Since then, variations have abounded, among them the habit of including candied peel, as here. We used mixed, pre-chopped peel. A gill is seldom used now—it is a ½ cup, but in fact this recipe benefits from a little less milk, as in our recipe below.

Mrs. Ayre's instructions about quickly changing oven temperatures indicate that this was a recipe intended for a gas or electric cookstove. The former arrived in Newfoundland in the first decade of the 20th century; the latter in the second. Although the source of this recipe is not known, it likely was a recipe published by a manufacturer as part of advertising the advantages of such stoves. However, having tried the two-temperature approach, there seems to be no advantage over baking at one temperature.

BATH BUNS
makes about 12 buns

1½ cups (225 g) flour
1 tablespoon (9 g) rice flour
2 teaspoons (10 g) baking powder
⅛ teaspoon (0.8 g) salt
4 tablespoons (30 g) minced candied peel

5 tablespoons (60 g) lard
6 tablespoons (90 ml) milk
5 tablespoons (60 g) sugar
1 egg
⅛ teaspoon (0.5 ml) vanilla

Preheat the oven to 350°F. Lightly grease a baking sheet, or use parchment or a silicone mat. Mix flour, rice flour, baking powder, and salt. Mix in the minced peel, breaking up any clumps. Gently heat the lard, milk, and sugar together until the sugar has dissolved and the lard has melted. Stir into the flour mixture. Whisk together the egg and vanilla, then mix with the previous mixture. Turn out and knead briefly to make a pliable dough. Roll into a long rope with your hands, and divide into 12 portions. Roll each portion into a little sphere, place on the prepared sheet, and flatten slightly to about 1 inch thick. Bake about 25 minutes, or until the buns are puffed up and lightly browned.

Pickavance & Murphy

76 Brandy Snaps

1 oz fat 1½ oz potato smooth ½ teasp ginger ½ oz sugar ½ oz syrup and about ¾ or 1 oz flour. Melt the fat syrup & sugar Stir in flour potatoes & ginger drop in little rounds on a baking tin – not close together mod. oven till rich brown.

There is no brandy in these brandy snaps and not much snap either. The instruction to space them out on the baking sheet indicates they were expected to spread out, like Ginger Snaps (112), for example, but this mixture does no such thing. If they were supposed to spread out, presumably a brittle brandy-snap texture was intended, which does not happen. We have given up on this recipe: either it is correct, in which case it is not worth making, or there are major flaws which can only be fixed by radically changing the recipe, which is beyond our self-imposed mandate to only tweak. So, for what it is worth, here is the original recipe. To be avoided.

Elsewhere (e.g., recipe 87) she qualifies syrup as corn syrup; the same is assumed here. The potato is mashed potato, mashed very smooth. Any fat can be used: lard, shortening, or butter all work well.

BRANDY SNAPS
makes 12

2 tablespoons (30 g) butter
2 teaspoons (10 ml) corn syrup
1 tablespoon (12.5 g) sugar
½ teaspoon (1.5 g) ginger
3 tablespoons (38 g) smooth mashed potato
3 tablespoons (30 g) flour

Preheat the oven to 350°F. Lightly grease a baking sheet, or use parchment paper or a silicone mat. Melt the butter in a small saucepan and sit in the syrup and sugar, then stir in the ginger and mashed potato, mashing any clumps until very smooth. Mash in the flour until the dough pulls away from the sides of the saucepan.

Turn out the dough, roll into a long rope, then divide into 12 equal portions. Roll each portion into a ball between your palms, then place on the prepared baking sheet, pressing each one down lightly into a fat disk. Bake about 20 minutes, or until well browned.

77 Rich Cocoanut Layer Cake

½ cup grated cocoanut ½ cup butter
1 cup sugar   2 eggs   ½ cup milk
2 cups flour 2 level teasp baking powder
Place on bottom rack in mod. oven
Bake 45 mins.   In 2 layers 25 mins
Put together with cocoanut frosting

As Mrs. Ayre suggests, this can be baked as two cakes, or as one which is cut in half horizontally. We baked it as one. The coconut frosting is not specified, so we made a butter-sugar one following contemporary sources. This makes a good coconut cake.

RICH COCONUT LAYER CAKE
makes one 8-inch (20 cm) round cake

½ cup (110 g) butter
1 cup (200 g) sugar
2 eggs
½ cup (45 g) desiccated coconut

2 cups (300 g) flour
2 teaspoons (10 g) baking powder
½ cup (125 ml) milk

Coconut frosting

2 cups (240 g) icing sugar
2 tablespoons (30 g) butter
4 teaspoons (20 ml) water or milk
½ cup (45 g) desiccated coconut
¼ teaspoon (1 ml) vanilla

Preheat the oven to 350°F. Grease and flour an 8-inch cake pan. Cream the butter and sugar together. Mix in the eggs and then the coconut. Mix the flour and baking powder, and stir this into the mixture alternately with milk. Scrape this batter into the prepared pan and smooth out the top. Bake for about 50 minutes, or until a small skewer inserted in the thickest part comes out clean. Turn out and cool on a rack. For the frosting: beat together the sugar, butter, and water to a stiff paste, then mix in the coconut and vanilla. If the frosting gets too stiff to spread, add an extra teaspoon of milk or water.

When the cake is cool, split it in half horizontally, spread the bottom half with the frosting, then cap with the top half.

78 Corn Bread.

¾ cup cornmeal
¾ cup flour   3 teasp baking powder
1 tablesp sugar   ⅓ teasp salt
¾ cup milk & water   2 tablesp bacon fat melted.

Bacon fat is particularly complementary to cornmeal-based dishes, but butter also works well. The original recipe calls for the fat to be melted before mixing in, but rubbing it into the dry mixture is fine.

This makes a shallow loaf, about 1½ inches thick. For a taller loaf, double the recipe and bake an extra 10 or 15 minutes. The loaf is crumbly and the slices are prone to falling apart, so the shallow loaf allows easier cutting.

Think of this loaf as a vehicle for toppings, such as butter and jam, and it is particularly good toasted and buttered while still warm.

CORN BREAD
makes one loaf

¾ cup (120 g) cornmeal
¾ cup (115 g) flour
3 teaspoons (15 g) baking powder
1 tablespoon (12.5 g) sugar
⅓ teaspoon (2 g) salt
2 tablespoons (30 g) bacon fat or butter
¾ cup (190 ml) equal parts milk and water

Preheat the oven to 350°F. Lightly grease a 4½ by 9-inch loaf pan. Mix the cornmeal, flour, baking powder, sugar, and salt. Melt the fat and drizzle it into the flour mixture, tossing it to distribute evenly. Stir in the milk and water to make a soft dough. Scrape into the prepared pan and smooth the top. Bake 25 to 30 minutes, or until the top is lightly browned, the cake is pulling away from the sides of the pan, and a small skewer inserted in the thickest part comes out clean. Turn out on a rack to cool.

79 Cornmeal Cakes

1 cup cornmeal
1 cup flour 1 teasp baking powder
2 tablesp shortening ½ cup sugar
1 cup raisins 1 egg ¼ cup milk

The original recipe does not have enough liquid, so we include more in our version. In the spirit of the plural title, this was baked as 6 small cakes, using large muffin pans, but it can be baked as one cake.

This makes a pleasant raisin bun (or cake), good with a cup of tea or as a snack at any time.

Pickavance & Murphy

CORNMEAL CAKES

makes 6 small cakes or one 8-inch (20 cm) round cake

1 cup (160 g) cornmeal
1 cup (150 g) flour
1 teaspoon (5 g) baking powder
½ cup (100 g) sugar

2 tablespoons (30 g) shortening or butter
1 cup (150 g) raisins
1 egg
½ cup (125 ml) milk

Preheat the oven to 350°F. Grease and flour 6 large muffin cups, each about 3½ inches across the top and 1¾ inches deep, or grease and flour an 8-inch cake pan.

Mix the cornmeal, flour, baking powder, and sugar, then rub in the shortening or butter until no lumps can be felt. Whisk the egg with the milk and stir into the dry mixture. Mix in the raisins. Divide the batter between the muffin cups, or put it all in the prepared pan. Bake the muffins about 25 to 30 minutes, the cake about 30 to 35 minutes, or in both cases until a small skewer inserted in the thickest part comes out clean.

80 Whole Wheat Muffins

1 cup whole wheat   ½ cup white flour
2 teasp baking powder 1 tablesp melted
butter 1 tablesp sugar 2 eggs (milk)
(red hot pan buttered sizzling)

The "red hot pan" is clearly hyperbolic, but what exactly is the recipe driving at here? Our best guess was something like the very hot pan with sizzling drippings used when making Yorkshire puddings. Grease the muffin pan before heating it to prevent the muffins sticking, or use a non-stick pan.

This makes a good basic savoury muffin, which is improved by a little salt.

WHOLE WHEAT MUFFINS
makes 6 muffins

1 cup (150 g) whole wheat flour
½ cup (75 g) white flour
2 teaspoons (10 g) baking powder
½ teaspoon (3.3 g) salt
2 tablespoons (30 g) butter, plus extra to grease the pan
1 tablespoon (12.5 g) sugar
2 eggs
⅔ cup (165 ml) milk

Preheat the oven to 450°F. Grease the sides of 6 standard muffin cups, each about 3 inches at the top and 1¼ inches deep. Divide 1 tablespoon butter into 6 pieces and place 1 piece in each muffin cup.

Mix the whole wheat flour, white flour, baking powder, and salt. Melt the butter. Whisk the eggs with the melted butter and milk, then stir into the dry mixture to make a smooth batter.

Put the prepared muffin pan in the oven for about 2 minutes, or until the butter is sizzling and starting to brown. Quickly divide the batter between the muffin cups, about ⅓ cup in each, and return to the oven. Bake about 15 minutes, or until a small skewer inserted in the thickest part of a muffin comes out clean. Turn out on a rack to cool.

81 Griddle Cakes

1 cup whole wheat flour
½ cup cornmeal   ½ cup bran ½ cup white flour   2 heaping teasp. b.powder
1 tablesp brown sugar   1 teasp salt
well sifted together. Beat 1 egg well add milk or part milk & water add to dry ingredients. Thin batter
Bake or fry as griddle cakes.

Likely the bran was wheat bran, but if this is hard to find, use oat bran or wheat germ. Although the recipe says to bake or fry the griddle cakes, do not bother baking them. They will cook in the oven—give them about 15 minutes at 400°F—but they do not brown, and they look and taste rather insipid. But when fried, these are excellent griddle cakes, much like an American-style pancake (not the British crêpe-like pancake). Like pancakes, eat them with some combination of butter, jam, syrup, and bacon.

GRIDDLE CAKES
makes about 18 cakes

1 cup (150 g) whole wheat flour
½ cup (75 g) flour
½ cup (55 g) bran or wheat germ
1 teaspoon (6.5 g) salt
1 tablespoon (10 g) brown sugar
4 teaspoons (20 g) baking powder

1 egg
2 cups (500 ml) milk, or equal parts milk and water, plus extra to thin the batter if needed
butter to grease the frying pan

Mix all the dry ingredients. Beat the egg with about half the milk and mix into the dry ingredients. Then stir in the rest of the milk to make a smooth batter thin enough to flow when dropped in a pan. If you are uncertain about this, pour about ¼ cup of batter onto a plate—it should spread out to about a 4-inch circle. If it does not, scrape that batter back into the main batch and stir in another tablespoon of milk or water. Repeat as necessary.

Heat a large cast-iron frying pan over medium heat. When hot, lightly grease the pan with butter. Drop ¼-cup portions of batter onto the hot pan. Fry about 90 seconds and then inspect the underside: it should be attractively browned. Flip over the cakes and cook the other side for another 90 seconds. The batter will thicken as it stands, so stir in teaspoons of liquid to thin it as necessary. Cook the cakes in batches according to the size of the pan; a 12-inch pan, for example, will fry three at once. Keep them warm while you cook the rest.

82 Macaroni or Spaghetti with Tomato

¼ pk macaroni in boiling salted water. When tender pour can tomato soup over it when it has been drained Salt & pepper bake 15 mins.

Most macaroni (see recipe 31) came in long lengths that had to be broken into shorter pieces. Use standard macaroni elbows.

What is a quarter package of macaroni? If the recipe was intended to serve 4 to 6, about 1 pound of pasta is required. A package must have been at least 4 pounds, if only a quarter of it is used. Trial and error taught us that this recipe needs a minimum of 4 cups of tomato soup, preferably 5 cups (1250 ml). Perhaps Mrs. Ayre's can of soup was a 2-pound can, which would have contained about 1 quart of soup.

In other macaroni recipes, Mrs. Ayre typically cooks the pasta for 20 minutes or more, far longer than the typical 10 minutes of today. In the spirit of the times, we cooked the pasta for the longer time.

As in any of the ubiquitous "now-add-a-can-of" pasta recipes, the quality of the

finished product depends entirely on the quality of the soup: an excellent, flavourful homemade soup will make a tasty dish; use a thin, low-grade soup, and the pasta will follow suit. But as real pasta sauces seem to be in everyone's repertoire today, this is a bit of an anachronism.

The time in the oven is designed both to reheat the pasta after it has cooled while draining and by the addition of cold soup and to give the pasta time to absorb some of the liquid. Both can also be achieved on top of the stove using a very low heat.

MACARONI OR SPAGHETTI WITH TOMATO
serves 4 to 6

3½ cups (450 g) macaroni
4 quarts (4 l) water
4 teaspoons (25 g) salt

4–5 cups (1–1.25 l) canned tomato soup, highest quality (or, better, use homemade)

Preheat the oven to 350°F. Bring the water to a boil in a 6-quart or larger saucepan. When boiling, add the salt and pasta, stir until it comes back to a boil, and cook for 20 minutes, stirring occasionally. Drain the pasta in a colander, shaking it around to help all surplus water drain away. Tip the drained pasta into a 4-quart casserole or baking dish, pour the soup over it and mix thoroughly. Bake for about 15 minutes.

To serve, scoop up from the bottom of the dish, where there will be a pool of soup—get some of this with each serving.

83 Lemon Snow

1 pt boiling water 1 cup sugar grated rind & juice 1 lemon 2 tablesp cornstarch dissolved in cold water   Boil till thicken add whites of 2 eggs well beaten. Pour into a mould serve cold with custard made yolks of eggs & flavoured vanilla

This recipe did not work on the first try; the mixture was too fluid to fold into the beaten egg whites. The key—and missing—information is that the 2 tablespoons of cornstarch in the original recipe should be *heaped* tablespoons, with as much above the bowl of the spoon as in it, which doubles the amount, as in our recipe below.

If you pour the finished mixture into a mould, as the recipe says, do not expect to turn it out; it does not set that firm. Any dish or mould can be used because the snow has to be spooned out.

Use the whites of the eggs in this recipe, and the yolks to make a custard (recipe 55) to serve with it. Not a particularly good dessert, but it might be a success at a children's birthday party.

LEMON SNOW
serves 4

2 cups (500 ml) water
1 cup (200 g) sugar
1 lemon, juice and grated zest
4 tablespoons (30 g) cornstarch
4 tablespoons (60 ml) cold water
2 eggs

Heat the 2 cups of water with the 1 cup of sugar in a 2-quart saucepan. Add the lemon zest and juice. Stir the cornstarch with the 4 tablespoons of water, mashing out any lumps until the starch is fully suspended, and stir into the pot. Whisk occasionally until the mixture comes to a boil and has thickened. Remove from the heat and cool; standing it in cold water will speed the process. Separate the eggs. When the mixture is cool and has set into semi-solid jelly, whisk it (or beat with a spoon) to break it up. Whip the egg whites to stiff peaks and fold them in, and scrape into a serving dish.

---

84 Fry boiled hominy

cut in strips in egg
& crumbs in fat. With bacon.

Hominy was widely available at the beginning of the 20th century—at least as cattle food, to judge by the advertisements in the press. But references to it as a breakfast food do exist, although we have no idea which grind was used. Coarse-ground hominy, in which the corn kernels are cracked into small rectangles, about ⅜ inch long, yields the best texture, but a finer grind is easier to handle. We used coarse ground, but it is difficult to get it to hold together while cutting and frying. Our approach was to presoak the hominy before simmering, which makes it hold together better after cooking. But be guided by whatever type you have and your own experience.

To make the crumbs, pound them in a plastic bag or pulse in a food processor. Pass them through a colander and re-pound (or re-process) the larger pieces.

FRIED HOMINY
serves 4

1 cup (190 g) coarse hominy
4 cups (1 l) water

1 teaspoon (6.5 g) salt

For frying

2 eggs
2 tablespoons (30 ml) milk
2 pinches (0.2 g) salt

1 cup (100 g) cracker crumbs, from about 10 crackers
3 tablespoons (37 g) lard (or vegetable oil)

Soak the hominy in excess water overnight. Drain, discard that water, and bring back to a boil in 4 cups of water with the teaspoon of salt. Simmer on a very low heat about 1½ hours. Drain any surplus water, then spread the boiled hominy in an 8 by 8-inch pan and cool completely.

Whisk the eggs with the milk and salt. Carefully cut the hominy into 8 rectangles—the

fewer cuts, the less likely it is to crumble and fall apart. Carefully lift the pieces from the pan with a thin spatula.

Heat the lard in a large cast-iron frying pan. Gently dip the rectangles of hominy in the beaten egg, and then in the crumbs, pressing the crumbs gently onto all surfaces. Fry the crumbed hominy on medium heat for 3 or 4 minutes on each side (turn them carefully), or until golden brown. Serve at once, ideally with bacon.

85 Baked Onions.

Cook onions until tender in 2 waters, 2nd water salted and boiling. drain well pressing each onion in a coarse cloth gently so as not to break it, and when they are dry, lay all together side by side in a bakepan. Pepper, salt & butter & add a cup of stock. Brown in a quick oven, take out the onions & keep them hot in a deep dish while you thicken gravy left in the pan with browned flour Pour over onions set in oven for a few minutes.

In the absence of other instructions, we used medium onions, each about 5 ounces untrimmed weight, 4 ounces trimmed weight. She does not specify if they are boiled peeled or unpeeled, and we were not convinced of the advantage of cooking twice. We tried boiling them peeled and unpeeled, once and twice, and found it is only necessary to boil them once, and it works better if they are not peeled.

BAKED ONIONS
serves 4 to 6

6 medium (about 900 g, whole untrimmed weight) onions
2 quarts (2 l) water
1 tablespoon (15 g) butter
salt and pepper to taste
1 cup (250 ml) beef or chicken stock
2 tablespoons (20 g) flour
¼ cup (60 ml) water

Bring 2 quarts of water to a boil in a 4-quart saucepan, drop in the whole, unpeeled onions, and bring back to a boil. Simmer about 30 minutes, then remove the onions and drop into cold water.

Preheat the oven to 400°F. When the onions are cool enough to handle, carefully trim the ends and gently peel away the outer brown skin and a layer of the inner onion. Sometimes the root end of the onion protrudes, so gently push it back into the onion. If there is excess water in the onion, wrap it in a cloth or layers of paper towel and gently squeeze.

Stand the peeled onions in a small baking dish or casserole that holds them comfortably, about 5 by 8 inches.

Pour the stock over the onions. Smear a piece of butter on the top of each onion, and sprinkle with salt and pepper. Bake for 45 to 60 minutes or until the tops of the onions are lightly browned and they are cooked (but a skewer stuck through the thickest part will still meet gentle resistance—onions cooked this way never get completely soft).

Remove the onions to a serving dish and keep warm. Pour all the cooking liquid into a small saucepan and bring to a simmer. Put the flour into a small jar with a lid, add ¼ cup of water, put on the lid and shake vigorously to make a lump-free suspension of flour. Whisk tablespoons of the flour mixture into the simmering cooking liquid until the desired consistency is reached. Simmer for 5 or 10 minutes, taste and adjust the seasoning, and pour over the reserved onions. Serve at once or put back in the oven briefly to reheat.

86 Nut Savoury.

2 oz ches nuts. 1 oz grated cheese   1 tablesp bread crumbs 4 tablesp mashed potatoes, a little milk, chopped parsley, pepper & salt. Mix together nuts cheese crumbs potatoes season well to taste. Add chopped parsley & make into stiff batter with butter milk. Put this mixture into a greased dish & bake in mod. oven for 20 mins.

A savoury was a small, tasty morsel served at the end of the meal as a digestive. Combinations of mushrooms or nuts were particularly favoured for their savouriness. They are not often served today, which is a pity because a small spoonful of something piquantly tasty does work as the finale of a large meal. A cheese course (when served after dessert) serves the same purpose.

For advice on peeling chestnuts, see recipe 20. Buttermilk adds to the savoury nature of this dish, but plain milk is fine.

NUT SAVOURY
serves 6 to 8

6 (about 60 g, peeled weight) chestnuts
⅓ cup (25 g) cheese
1 tablespoon (5 g) bread crumbs
4 tablespoons (50 g) mashed potato

salt and pepper to taste
2 tablespoons (8 g) chopped parsley
3 tablespoons (45 ml) buttermilk

Preheat the oven to 350°F. Grease a 4 by 6-inch baking dish. Grate the cheese. Peel the chestnuts and chop coarsely to no more than about ¼-inch dice. Mix with the grated cheese, bread crumbs, and mashed potatoes, and season to taste. Stir in the chopped parsley and buttermilk to make a stiff paste. Scrape into the prepared dish, level, and bake about 20 minutes. Serve small portions at the end of a formal dinner.

87. Potato Apple Pudding.

1 lb apples – core
¼ cup corn syrup, 1 cup cooked potatoes
2 eggs, 2 tablesp flour, a little cinnamon
1 tablesp lemon juice & a little of
the lemon rind grated 2 tablesp
butter. Stew apples with syrup until
tender mash potatoes & put with apple
add melted butter, beaten eggs, flour
spice & lemon juice. Bake in a well
greased pan 35 mins. This pudding
may be changed by adding yolks
only. Bake until firm. Beat whites
stiff add 1 tablesp brown sugar ½ teasp
vanilla pile on pudding & brown in oven

Any apple can be used, but a better final texture results if the apples do not fall apart: use Granny Smith or Golden Delicious or similarly firm apple.

POTATO APPLE PUDDING
serves 4

3 medium (about 500 g, whole weight) apples
¼ cup (60 ml) corn syrup
1 cup (200 g) mashed potato
2 tablespoons (30 g) butter
2 eggs
2 tablespoons (20 g) flour
⅛ teaspoon (0.4 g) cinnamon
1 tablespoon (15 ml) lemon juice
½ teaspoon (0.7 g) grated lemon zest

For the alternative version
1 tablespoon (10 g) brown sugar
½ teaspoon (2.5 ml) vanilla

Preheat the oven to 350°F. Grease a 1-quart pie dish or baking pan. Peel, core, and coarsely chop the apples. Put them and the syrup into a saucepan and bring to a boil. Simmer about 10 to 15 minutes or until the apples are completely soft. Pour the juices from the cooked apples into the mashed potato, mix well to loosen the potato, then pour back with the apples and mix well.

Melt the butter and let cool. Beat the eggs, whisk in the cool (but liquid) butter, the flour, cinnamon, lemon juice, and zest. Mix into the apple and potato mixture. Scrape the batter into the prepared dish. Bake 30 to 40 minutes, or until the top is lightly browned, with darker edges.

For the alternative version, proceed as above except separate the eggs and use only the yolks in the initial batter. When the pudding is done, beat the egg whites to soft peaks, then add the brown sugar and vanilla and beat the mixture to stiff peaks. Spread evenly on the baked pudding and put back in the oven for about 10 minutes to brown.

Evening Telegram, February 21, 1918.

88. Blueberry Muffins.

2 cups rice flour
or 1 cup potato flour, 1 cup corn flour
½ teasp salt   3 tablesp sugar 3 teasp baking powder 1½ to 2 cups milk
2 tablesp butter 1½ cups blueberries
1 egg - Sift dry ingredients add beaten egg & enough milk to make thick batter. Beat well add melted butter & blueberries which have been dusted with flour Bake in muffin tins in a hot oven 20 - 30 mins

Use rice flour. That amount of potato flour does not work. There is a little too much milk in this recipe, so it was reduced accordingly. We used standard muffin pans, each cup about 3 inches across the top and 1¼ inches deep.

BLUEBERRY MUFFINS
makes 12 muffins

2 cups (280 g) rice flour
1 cup (120 g) corn flour
½ teaspoon (3.3 g) salt
3 tablespoons (38 g) sugar
3 teaspoons (15 g) baking powder

1 egg
1¼ – 1½ cups (312 – 375 ml) milk
2 tablespoons (30 g) butter
1½ cups (180 g) blueberries
2 tablespoons (20 g) flour

Preheat the oven to 400°F. Grease a standard 12-cup muffin pan. Mix the dry ingredients (but not the blueberries). Melt the butter and let it cool, but do not let it set. Beat the egg, whisk in the cool but liquid butter, then stir into the dry ingredients, alternating with portions of milk. Start with the lesser amount of milk, then add tablespoons of the last ¼ cup to make a batter that will reluctantly pour off a spoon. Roll the blueberries in the 2 tablespoons of flour, shake off the surplus in a sieve, then fold into the batter. Divide the batter between the prepared muffin cups. Bake about 20 minutes, or until the muffins are risen, slightly browned, cracked on top, and a small skewer inserted into the thickest part comes out clean. Turn out on a rack to cool.

89 Split pea soup.

Soak two cups of split peas over night. Next morning put them on to boil. Take 1 sm onion 1 sm turnip 1 carrot slice and fry brown add them & let all boil together until dinner time. Strain and add to the liquor pieces of bread cut and fried brown.

Mrs. Ayre likely meant split yellow peas, by far the more common in the stores of her day, but this soup is equally good made with split green peas. This is one of the few recipes for "ordinary" food in Mrs. Ayre's notebook. But it is an unusual pea soup—at least for Newfoundland—because it contains no meat; it may have been included for the edification of the household cook, who would likely have routinely cooked pea soup with hunks of salt meat.

Boiling the soup from breakfast to dinner (presumably midday) is excessive; it needs at most 90 minutes. The intention behind straining the soup is that the soup and vegetable are rubbed through a sieve, which is not as onerous as it sounds, because the vegetables are very soft after a long simmering. A blender will do the work in seconds, although the product is more finely textured than when it is sieved.

The bread cubes are croutons. Either fry them, as indicated in the original recipe, or bake them, a far better method because the croutons get much more evenly browned and dry out to a much crisper texture.

The soup can be kept for use another day, but it will thicken considerably as it stands, so reheat gently with at least an extra cup of water and more salt to taste.

SPLIT PEA SOUP
makes at least 2 quarts (2 l) of thick soup

- 2 cups (400 g) split yellow peas
- 2 quarts (2 l) water
- 1 small (about 100 g) onion
- 1 small (about 250 g) or ½ medium (about 500 g) turnip
- 1 medium (about 100 g) carrot
- 2 tablespoons (30 g) butter
- 1½ teaspoons (10 g) salt, plus more to taste
- 2 slices (each about 4 x 6 inches/ 10 x 15 cm) bread
- 1 tablespoon melted butter or oil to fry/bake the bread cubes

Soak the dried peas in excess water overnight or for at least 12 hours and then drain. Bring 2 quarts of water to a boil, add the soaked, drained peas, bring back to a boil and simmer about 1½ hours. Peel the vegetables and slice or coarsely chop them. Fry the vegetables in 2 tablespoons of butter in a frying pan or wide saucepan on a medium heat. Fry for the first 5 minutes with the cover on, then about another 5 minutes until the vegetables are browning at the edges. Tip these and any remaining butter into the simmering soup at around the 1-hour mark. Add the salt.

After simmering 1½ hours, pour the soup in batches into a coarse sieve and rub it through with a stiff rubber spatula (or blend). Reheat and add extra water and salt as needed.

Make the croutons while the soup reheats. Remove the crusts and cut the slices of bread into ½- to ¾-inch cubes. Each slice of bread will yield around 35 cubes. Toss with the melted butter or oil. Fry or bake the bread cubes. To fry, spread the cubes out in a large frying pan on low-medium heat and fry for 10 to 15 minutes, turning frequently to brown all sides. Baking the bread cubes gives a better result: preheat the oven to 350°F. Spread the cubes in a single layer on a baking sheet. Bake about 25 minutes, turning after 10 minutes and every 5 minutes thereafter with a wide spatula, dragging those at the periphery to the centre. Be careful: after about 20 to 25 minutes the croutons will go from undercooked to burnt quickly. As soon as they look nearly done, turn them over about every 2 minutes until browned to your satisfaction.

Serve bowls of soup with a few croutons sprinkled on top at the very last moment because they go soggy very quickly.

90 – Cornmeal Fritter

1 cup cornmeal
1 cup flour   2 tablesps fat   1 egg
1 tablesp sugar 2 heaping teasp baking powder, mix all together with milk & water, fry in hot lard & serve with sweet sauce.

These are essentially cornmeal pancakes in the American tradition. This was probably a breakfast dish, although it may have been a dessert. Any sweet sauce can be used, but we suggest the traditional Newfoundland molasses sauce below.

CORNMEAL FRITTERS
serves 4 to 6

1 cup (160 g) cornmeal
1 cup (150 g) flour
2 tablespoons (30 g) butter
1 egg
1 tablespoon (12.5 g) sugar
4 teaspoons (20 g) baking powder

1¼–1½ cups (315–375 ml) milk and water mixed
2 tablespoons (30 g) lard or butter for frying
sweet sauce to serve

For the sweet sauce: molasses sauce (lassy coady)

1 cup (250 ml) molasses
2 tablespoons (30 g) butter
¼ teaspoon (0.75 g) cinnamon

Make the sauce ahead of time: heat the sauce ingredients together and stir well to combine; reserve and keep warm.

Mix the cornmeal and flour. Melt the butter, whisk the egg, and mix these into the cornmeal and flour. Stir in the lesser amount of milk and water, then add extra milk/water as needed to make a loose, just pourable, pancake batter.

Heat a 12-inch cast-iron frying pan on low-medium heat. When hot, melt a teaspoon of the lard for frying. Drop approximately ¼-cup portions of the batter into the pan—there will be room for 3 or 4. Fry 1 to 1½ minutes, or until nicely patterned with brown, then flip the fritters over and fry the other side for the same time. Keep fried fritters warm while frying the rest. Add more teaspoons of lard as required. If the batter thickens, thin with a little extra milk. Serve with the molasses sauce on the side or poured over.

91 Chowder.

Dice 3 large potatoes & 1 large onion & slice one 3 lb fish or use 3 lbs of cutlets – Have bacon dripping hot & brown all but fish in it until crisp and well coloured. Have a deep saucepan & baking dish ready & fill it with layers of potatoes   broken ship's crakers or water biscuit, onion & fish - Bits of salt pork should also be Mixed in. Season each layer to just taste & when all is in pour on boiling water to almost cover it. Simmer it gently 20 minutes. Arrange chowder in mound on plate garnish with minced parsley & pour ½ pint thickened milk seasoned with butter pepper & salt over whole Serve very hot with fresh brown bread boiled beets & hot coffee

With clams use Ships crackers. Some cooks use tomato seasoning.

What is a large potato? A large onion? As elsewhere, we take approximately 8 ounces whole, unpeeled weight for both. Bacon dripping (rendered bacon fat) lends a savoury edge to this dish, but plain butter works as well. To make the crumbs, pound the crackers in a plastic bag with a rolling pin. Less historically accurate but more efficient is brief pulsing in a food processor.

Salt pork is good, but regular streaky bacon also works well and may be more to many people's taste. In accordance with Newfoundland usage, fish in this context is codfish. The amount is flexible, but after allowing for skin, bones, and wastage of a whole 3-pound fish, we arrived at about 2 pounds trimmed weight fish fillet.

The tricky part is making sure the potatoes get cooked at the same time as the fish. Cut them into small pieces, and simmer before adding the fish, as described below.

Be careful heating the saucepan after the cracker crumbs have been added; because they absorb much of the liquid, there is risk of scorching.

Do not be fussy about the layering in the pot—it is all going to get jumbled up when spooned out onto the platter, so the description below is for convenience.

The plate on which you turn out the chowder must be big and deep enough to hold the solids and the thickened milk. We used a 12 by 16-inch oval platter, one where the rim is raised about 1½ inches above the table surface.

As the recipe suggests, this is indeed good with fresh, brown bread, preferably straight out of the oven and generously buttered. Boiled beets and coffee with this may be to your taste, but they were not to ours.

CHOWDER

serves 6 to 8

- 15 (150 g) crackers
- ⅓ cup (50 g) salt pork or fatty bacon
- 4 cups (1 kg) trimmed cod fillet
- 3 large (750 g, total whole weight) potatoes
- 1 large (250 g, whole weight) onion
- 2 tablespoons (30 g) bacon drippings or butter
- salt and pepper to taste
- 3 cups (750 ml) boiling water
- ½ cup (30 g) parsley for garnish

For the thickened milk

- 1 tablespoon (15 g) butter
- 1 tablespoon (10 g) flour
- 1 cup (250 ml) milk
- salt and pepper to taste

Crush the crackers into crumbs. Dice the salt pork or bacon into ⅛-inch cubes. Cut the fish into 2-inch chunks. Peel the potatoes and onion, and dice into about ½-inch pieces. Heat the drippings or butter in a wide, 4-quart saucepan and fry the potato and onion together until the onion is translucent and beginning to brown at the edges. Add about 2 cups boiling water, season lightly, cover and simmer for a few minutes until the potatoes

are just cooked through but not falling apart. Gently stir in the crumbs and the pork or bacon dice. Add the chunks of fish, season lightly again, and add about another cup of boiling water or enough to almost cover the fish. Bring slowly back to a gentle boil, and simmer with the cover on about 20 minutes. Inspect the fish, and if there is any hint of rawness, simmer another 5 or more minutes until the fish is completely cooked.

Meanwhile, make the thickened milk sauce. Melt the butter in a small saucepan, stir in the flour, whisk in the milk, and bring to a boil. Simmer about 5 minutes, then season to taste.

When the fish is cooked, ladle the chowder out onto an appropriate platter, pour the milk sauce over it, and sprinkle with the chopped parsley. Serve immediately.

92 Delicious Pudding.

1 breakfast cup breadcrumbs ½ either prunes (soaked & chopped) or raisins or dates. 2 tablesp tapioca soaked in milk or water all night. 2 table brown sugar [1 ?] tablesp butter or dripping ½ teasp soda - Steam 2 ½ hours

Opinions differ about the size of breakfast cups, but the general consensus is that they are bigger than a standard cup, because everyone needs a *big* cup of coffee or tea at breakfast time. The one we used was about 10 ounces (1¼ cups). The bread crumbs are the moist, fresh variety; fine, dry crumbs will make this unpalatably soggy.

Tapioca is discussed in recipe 24. This recipe refers to larger spheres of tapioca that need soaking overnight. But the smaller, granular tapioca (like coarse sugar) is much more easily available; we adapted this recipe for that form.

Calling this pudding "delicious" is a stretch; it is an unremarkable pudding.

DELICIOUS PUDDING
serves 4

2 tablespoons (24 g) granular tapioca
1 cup (250 ml) water
1 tablespoon (15 g) butter or drippings
1¼ cups (100 g) fresh bread crumbs

2 tablespoons (20 g) brown sugar
½ teaspoon (2.5 g) baking soda
½ cup (75 g) raisins, prunes, or dates

Soak the tapioca in the water in a small saucepan for about 10 minutes, then bring to a boil and simmer about 5 minutes, or until it has gone completely translucent. Set aside to cool slightly. Grease a 1½-quart (1.5 l) pudding basin.

Melt the butter and toss with the crumbs. Mix the soda with the sugar, mashing out any lumps, and then mix in the raisins, separating any clumps. Mix with the buttered crumbs. While the tapioca is still warm, fold it into the mixture. Scrape the batter into the prepared pudding basin, tie a cloth over the top, and steam for about 1½ hours. Do not let the steamer boil dry: check the water level every half hour or so, and add boiling water as necessary.

> *93 Parkins*
>
> *2 lbs oatmeal ½ lb brown*
> *sugar   6 oz dripping   1 oz best ground ginger*
> *crumble all together mix to stiff dough*
> *with little molasses.   Roll out*
> *cut into squares & bake on a tin*
> *- quick oven 15 to 20 mins.*

This is from northern Britain. In the north of England it is called parkin, while in Scotland it is often perkins; perhaps Mrs. Ayre's parkins was a corruption of a Scottish recipe.

This version resembles the original parkin, a dense, unleavened griddle cake. When baking powder became readily available, parkin became a much lighter, leavened cake. In Britain parkin became particularly associated with November 5, bonfire night, or Guy Fawkes night.

The full recipe makes a lot of parkin, so the version we give below is half the original.

The instruction to cut into squares before baking is problematic because the mixture spreads extensively as it bakes, which obscures any cuts you have made. A better approach is to cut the rolled mixture into about 8 pieces, then bake these 4 at a time, spaced out on a baking sheet where they will flow together into one sheet. After they have been out of the oven for a few minutes but are still pliable, score them directly in the baking sheet into the desired size. When they are cool and set, lift out with a metal spatula, folding them to break along the scores if they have welded themselves together.

PARKINS
serves 6

3 cups (450 g) oatmeal
¾ cup (115 g) brown sugar
6 tablespoons (90 g) drippings or lard

5½ tablespoons (30 g) ginger
½ cup (125 ml) molasses

Preheat the oven to 400°F. Lightly grease 2 large baking sheets, about 12 by 16 inches, or use parchment paper or a silicone mat. Rub the fat into the oatmeal until completely absorbed. Mix in the sugar and ginger. Mix in the molasses. Roll out the mixture to a rectangle about 9 by 12 inches, about ⅜ inch thick. Cut this roughly into 8 pieces, and space 4 out on each baking sheet. Bake 8 or 9 minutes, or until the mixture has spread and merged and bubbles in places. Remove the sheets from the oven and cool for 7 or 8 minutes. While still warm and pliable, score into the desired sizes. When cold and set, lift out the pieces with a spatula, breaking apart as necessary.

94 Dainty Pudding (economical)

Put into a basin a heaped teacup flour pinch salt 1 tablesp sugar 1 ½ margarine or butter Mix all well together and add a tablesp jam lastly add teasp soda mixed in ¼ teacup warm water Stir well put in a well greased basin with a little jam at the bottom. Cover with greased paper steam 1 ½ hrs Enough for 6.

How big was her teacup? And how high was it heaped? After experimentation, it seems that it equalled a standard 8-ounce cup. Somehow, though, the necessary liquid—milk or water—got forgotten; we put it back.

Use any jam, but preferably one rich in fruit acids (e.g., partridgeberry or cranberry) that will provide the acidity to make the soda work.

The greased paper cover on the pudding is not necessary, but tying a cloth over the basin definitely is, because it stops condensation from dripping onto the pudding as it steams.

Despite the unpromising title—we view anything labelled "economical" with suspicion—this is a pleasant pudding, and if made with a tangy jam, makes a welcome dessert.

DAINTY PUDDING (ECONOMICAL)
serves 6

1 cup (150 g) flour
1 pinch (0.1g) salt
1 tablespoon (12.5 g) sugar
1½ tablespoons (23 g) butter or margarine
3 tablespoons (45 ml) jam
1 teaspoon (5 g) baking soda
2 tablespoons (30 ml) warm water
½ cup (125 ml) milk

Grease a 1½-quart pudding basin. Mix the flour, salt, and sugar. Rub in the butter until it is all absorbed. Suspend the soda in the warm (not hot) water, and stir into the mixture. Stir in 1 tablespoon of jam. Spread the other 2 tablespoons of jam in the bottom of the prepared basin, then scrape the mixture gently on top and smooth the top, trying not to disturb the layer of jam underneath too much.

Cover with a circle of greased or parchment paper (optional). Tie a cloth over the top of the basin and steam for 1½ hours. Do not let the steamer boil dry; check the level every half hour or so and add boiling water as necessary.

95 Cheese

Mix 3 tablesp dried grated cheese with yolks of 2 eggs & 2 tablesps fresh butter or salad oil Season with pinch cayenne & salt Toast bread & spread above mixture on it thickly. Put slices in a dish or pan with tight cover & place in oven until hot through. Now take off cover and brown lightly

This rich variant of toasted cheese or Welsh rabbit (recipe 60) makes enough for two generous helpings, and can easily be stretched to make three or even four.

Butter is much better than salad oil (olive oil) in this recipe, but make sure that it is very soft so that it mixes easily with the other ingredients. If the butter is hard, melt it and then let it cool to room temperature until it just starts to solidify.

The fussy procedure of baking the toasts covered and then uncovered is not necessary. Simply bake them uncovered for the requisite time.

CHEESE
serves 2

2 egg yolks
2 tablespoons (30 g) soft butter
pinch (0.1 g) cayenne
pinch (0.1 g) salt
3 tablespoons (15 g) grated cheese
2 slices bread

Preheat the oven to 400°F. Beat the butter into the yolks, then mix in the cayenne, salt, and cheese. Toast the bread. Divide the cheese mixture between the slices of toast and spread it out over the slice. Place them on a baking sheet and bake 16 to 18 minutes, or until the cheese is puffed and browning in patches. Serve immediately.

---

96 Nut Bread

4 tablesp butter 1 cup sugar
1 cup milk 4 cups flour 2 eggs
2 teasp baking powder 1 cup (or more)
chopped nuts. Rise for 20 mins

The 1 cup of milk in the original recipe is not enough; it needs at least an extra ¼ cup to make a manageable dough. No doubt any nuts could be used; we used pecans, coarsely chopped.

The instruction to rise for 20 minutes is confusing. It sounds like the preliminary rising of a yeast-leavened bread, but that does not apply here since this one uses baking powder. And it can hardly mean baking time, because almost three times that is needed.

Makes a very pleasant, mild nut bread, a great vehicle for butter and jam.

NUT BREAD
makes 1 loaf

4 tablespoons (60 g) butter
1 cup (200 g) sugar
2 eggs
4 cups (600 g) flour

2 teaspoons (10 g) baking powder
1¼ cups (315 ml) milk
1 cup (100 g) pecans or other nuts

Preheat the oven to 350°F. Grease a 5 by 10-inch loaf pan. Chop the nuts coarsely. Cream together the butter and sugar. Mix in the eggs. Mix the baking powder with the flour, and stir this into the mixture, alternating with the milk. When well mixed, fold in the chopped nuts. Scrape into the prepared pan, smooth the top with damp fingers, and bake 60 to 70 minutes, or until the top is browned and a small skewer inserted in the thickest part comes out clean.

97 Jelly Roll.

2 yolks beaten stiff then add ½ cup sugar. Beat 10 minutes
Next add ½ cup flour sifted with small teasp baking powder. Add 2 whites beaten stiff.

This is obviously just the cake part of a jelly roll, the thin layer of which is rolled around a sweet filling. The filling part is not dealt with by Mrs. Ayre.

There are two difficulties. First, the mixture of yolks, sugar, and flour is so stiff and crumbly that it is impossible to fold in the whipped egg whites successfully—adding a little milk solves that problem. The second difficulty is more severe: even with precautions, the baked cake layer tends to stick. The old-fashioned grease and flour method is perhaps the best preventative, but even then the cake is tricky to remove from the pan. Modern methods like parchment paper are less efficient, and the batter even sticks to a silicone mat. Be very careful when getting the cake layer out of its pan.

There is no need to beat the yolks and sugar for 10 minutes; just make sure they are well combined and a pale yellow before adding the milk.

JELLY ROLL
makes the cake part of one jelly roll

2 eggs
½ cup (100 g) sugar
2 tablespoons (30 ml) milk

½ cup (75 g) flour
½ teaspoon (2.5 g) baking powder

Preheat the oven to 350°F. Liberally grease and flour a 10 by 14-inch baking sheet. Separate the eggs. Whisk the yolks and sugar together until pale yellow. Whisk in the milk. Mix the flour and baking powder, and stir them into the yolk mixture until homogeneous. Beat the egg whites to stiff peaks and fold into the mixture. Spread over the prepared baking sheet, making it as even as possible. Bake 12 to 14 minutes or until the top is light brown. Let cool out of the oven for a few minutes before very carefully separating the cake layer from the pan with the aid of two wide spatulas. Reserve and use to make a jelly roll.

98 Cheese Souffle

2 tablespoons butter   3 level tables flour
½ cup scalded milk   ½ teasp salt
½ cup grated cheese   2 eggs (or 3)
Melt butter add flour then milk
& cheese   Take off the fire & add
yolks, cool. Then stir in
whipped whites   bake ½ hour
& serve at once in same pie dish

The extra lifting power of the third egg white makes this soufflé puff up more, so use the 3-egg option. The only point of scalding the milk is to speed the process, but with only ½ cup of milk, the time saved is minimal; there is an extra pot to wash, so use cold milk. Use a sharp cheddar. Since such cheese is already salty, reduce the salt, as in our recipe below.

When the whipped whites are folded into the cheese sauce, it helps to first stir in about ⅓ cup to lighten the mixture, and then proceed to fold in the rest. We made this in a pudding basin, but any similar-sized ovenproof container can be used.

CHEESE SOUFFLÉ
serves 4

2 tablespoons (30 g) butter
3 tablespoons (30 g) flour
½ cup (125 ml) milk
¼ teaspoon (1.5 g) salt
½ cup (37 g) grated cheese
3 eggs

Preheat the oven to 400°F. Grease and flour a 1½-quart dish. Separate the eggs. Melt the butter in a small saucepan. Stir in the flour to make a smooth paste. Stir in the milk and heat until it thickens, stirring frequently. Take off the heat and stir in the cheese; much of it will melt, but it does not matter if small bits do not. Stir in the egg yolks. Whip the whites to stiff peaks and fold them into the cheese sauce. Scrape and pour into the prepared dish. Bake 35 to 40 minutes, or until the top is well browned. When it is taken out of the oven, the soufflé will deflate very quickly, so serve immediately.

99 Tomato Pickle

10 lb green tomatoes
4 large onions
Cut in slices sprinkle each
Layer with little salt, let stand
Overnight, in the morning drain
off water put on to boil with
1 qt. vinegar and 1 qt water boil
about 15 minutes & drain again
Put on again with – 1 qt vinegar
2 lbs sugar 1 dessertsp cinnamon
1 teasp. allspice 1 teasp ginger
Boil until tender

This seems an unnecessarily long-winded procedure. The initial salting does remove surplus water, but this could as easily be achieved by more simmering at the end. And what is the purpose of the first boiling, discarding the liquid, and then adding the same amount of vinegar for the second boiling? The final instruction to boil until tender does not make much sense because everything is soft already. Although the same result might be achieved more simply, we report the full process here for historical accuracy.

A dessertspoon is a bit less than a tablespoon, about 2½ teaspoons.

The result is a very good tomato pickle—more of a chutney, with the spices, salt, sugar, and vinegar perfectly balanced.

This recipe, after reducing as we recommend in our recipe, fills about seven 2-cup Mason jars to the neck. If a runny pickle is preferred, do not reduce it so much and stretch it over 8 jars.

TOMATO PICKLE
makes about 3 quarts (3 l)

10 pounds (4.5 kg) green tomatoes
4 large (about 1 kg, total unpeeled weight) onions
¾ cup (190 g) coarse pickling salt
8 cups (2 l) vinegar
4 cups (1 l) water
4½ cups (900 g) sugar
2½ teaspoons (7.5 g) cinnamon
1 teaspoon (3 g) allspice
1 teaspoon (3 g) ginger

Peel and slice the onions. Slice the tomatoes. Layer in a large, non-reactive saucepan, sprinkling the salt between the layers. Leave for 12 hours. Drain. Put the solids back in the saucepan, add half the vinegar and all the water, bring to a boil and simmer 15 minutes. Drain again, return the solids to the saucepan, add the other half of the vinegar, the sugar, and the spices, and bring back to a boil. Simmer until the desired thickness is reached. Simmer gently for 1 hour to reduce by 25 per cent. Ladle into jars.

100 Pickled Onions

Make a brine with 1 ½ cups salt and 2 qts boiling water let stand 2 days, drain, cover with more brine. Let stand 2 days longer. Make more brine heat to boiling point then put onions in to boil for 3 minutes. Put in hot jars with spice. Fill jars overflowing with vinegar scalded with sugar Allow 1 cup sugar to 1 gal vinegar

Small pickling onions (about 32 per lb) are best for this recipe, and although they are tedious to peel, it is worth the effort. Do not tackle them like regular onions. Instead, drop the pickling onions, whole and unpeeled, directly into boiling water. When the water returns to a boil, drain and plunge them into cold water. Nick the side of each onion with a small knife and slip off the outer layer or two. To help the onion stay together, leave a nub at the root end, and only trim any withered bits at the leaf end.

The recipe does not specify the quantity of onions, but the amount of brine in the recipe is enough for 4 or 5 pounds of small onions. One gallon of vinegar is far more than needed for this quantity of onions—it is simply an indication of the sugar/vinegar proportion. The amount required for the onions used here is given in our recipe below.

The spices are not specified, so we settled on equal parts of cinnamon, nutmeg, and cloves, entirely typical of the time.

This makes an excellent pickled onion, a suitable partner for cheese or many cold meats.

PICKLED ONIONS
fills six 2-cup Mason jars

4½ cups (1.125 kg) coarse pickling salt
6 quarts (6 l) water
4–5 pounds (1.8–2.25 kg untrimmed weight) small pickling onions
1½ teaspoons (4.5 g) mixed spices
10 cups (2.5 l) vinegar
1¼ cups (250 g) sugar

Bring the water to a boil, pour in the salt, and take off the heat. Stir occasionally. Peel the onions and place in a container with a lid. When all the salt has dissolved, pour about one-third of the salt solution over the peeled onions, enough to barely cover them. Put on the lid, and let stand at room temperature for 48 hours. Reserve the remaining brine.

After 48 hours, drain the onions and discard that part of the brine. Pour half of the reserved brine over the onions, replace the lid, and leave for another 48 hours.

After the second 48 hours, drain the onions again (and again discard that part of the brine), put them in a saucepan, add the last portion of reserved brine, bring to a boil, and simmer for 3 minutes.

Drain the onions again (again discarding the brine) and divide them between the jars. Sprinkle ¼ teaspoon of spices in each jar. Bring the vinegar and sugar to a boil, make sure the sugar is fully dissolved, then pour enough into each jar to cover the onions, reserving the surplus to top up the jars as they cool.

101 Tea buns

2 cups flour 2 heaping teasps baking powder 1 teasp sugar 2 tablesps butter. Roll out & plait.

An unusual recipe. It starts off like an ordinary tea bun, although it omits the necessary milk or water. But a plaited, challah-like tea bun? Definitely not mainstream. The method below is our interpretation of her rather laconic instruction.

TEA BUNS
serves 6 or more

2 cups (300 g) flour
2 tablespoons (30 g) butter
1 teaspoon (4 g) sugar

4 teaspoons (20 g) baking powder
¾ cup (190 ml) milk or water

Preheat the oven to 350°F. Lightly grease (or use parchment or a silicone mat) a baking sheet, at least 16 inches long. Rub the butter into the flour until it is all absorbed. Mix in the sugar and baking powder. Stir in the milk or water. Turn out on a lightly floured surface and fold it over and press together two or three times to incorporate all the loose pieces.

Roll or press the dough into a long rectangle, about 5 by 15 inches. Cut this lengthways into 3 equal strips. Lay these strips alongside each other on the baking sheet. Press the strips together at one end, then plait: fold the outside strip over the middle strip, alternately from each side. At the other end, press the strips together.

Bake 40 to 45 minutes, or until the top is lightly browned.

---

102 Whort Jam

4 lb whortz   1 lb sugar
1 teasp salt. Boil until jam.

Although *whort* in Newfoundland dialect can mean any of the various blueberries and bilberries, here it surely meant *the* common blueberry of Newfoundland, *Vaccinium angustifolium*. In season, these are plentiful, and were very popular made into jam, both for its own sake and as a means of keeping quantities of berries over the winter.

This recipe is a model of brevity; in fact, not much more is required. Simmer the berries until reduced to your liking, but remember that, when cool, they will thicken considerably, or cook to a setting-solid temperature of 220°F.

WHORT JAM
makes 6 to 8 cups (1.5 to 2 l) jam

4 pounds (1800 g) blueberries **1 teaspoon (6.5 g) salt**
1 pound (450 g) sugar

Mix the berries, salt, and sugar together in a large saucepan. Bring very slowly to a boil to avoid scorching as the berries release their juices, and simmer until the mixture has thickened to your liking or reached setting temperature.

---

103 Sterilized Rhubarb

Sterilize bottles 10 minutes Rubbers not so long. Blanch by dipping in cheesecloth bag in boiling water for 2 minutes & then in cold. Shake in bottles. Fill with boiling water 2 spoons of sugar. Shake down. Boil 16 minutes

---

This recipe is called canned rhubarb in the list at the beginning, so clearly it is bottling by other names (for general remarks, see recipe 71). The preliminary blanching of rhubarb is in line with modern techniques of about 1 to 2 minutes in boiling water before plunging into cold water. The timing is important: we gave it 2 minutes from the moment the rhubarb went into water at a full, rolling boil. A cheesecloth bag works for blanching, but it is easier to use a large sieve or a large slotted scoop.

Rhubarb expands more than expected in the processing, so leave more headroom in the jars than is usual for fruits and vegetables, at least 1 inch. As Mrs. Ayre has previously recommended, poke a spoon handle down inside each jar to agitate the contents to dislodge any air bubbles.

The minimal amount of sugar means that more can be added to taste at point of use.

STERILIZED RHUBARB (bottled rhubarb)
fills three 2-cup (500 ml) Mason jars

2 pounds (900 g) rhubarb **6 tablespoons (75 g) sugar**
water as needed

Slice the rhubarb into ½-inch pieces and blanch. Put them into the jars, leaving at least 1 inch of headroom below the rim. Remove air bubbles. Put 2 tablespoons of sugar in each jar, then pour in enough water to barely reach the top of the rhubarb, about ⅓ to ½ cup in each. Put on lids and threaded rings. Process in a boiling water bath.

Evening Telegram, July 6, 1917.

104 Fish Rolls in Custard

About 2 lb of fresh haddock
1 egg   ¾ pt milk   lemon juice &
chopped parsley.
I filleted my haddock & curled
Fillets into little rolls, which I stood
on end in a white fireproof dish.
Each of the rolls had to be sprinkled
over with lemon juice, pepper & salt
and a little chopped parsley. I
beat up the egg with the milk, and
set it ready to pour over the fish
when I should come to bake it
Takes ½ hour. Medium oven. Custard set.

The haddock are obviously small ones which yield 2 fillets, around ¼ pound each. These are often available frozen, but fresh are better.

Use a baking dish that holds the rolled fillets snugly. We used an oval pie dish, about 6 by 8 inches at the top. A baking dish of this size does not need the amount of milk in the recipe, so we have reduced it in our recipe below.

Roll the fillets skin side on the inside, which means that any curling during cooking favours the roll rather than trying to unroll it. And although not specified in the recipe, it helps to push a toothpick through each rolled-up fillet to hold it rolled while you fit them in the dish.

Not a very satisfactory recipe. The custard only sets properly around the edges of the dish because the fish oozes liquid as it cooks, which dilutes the custard in the immediate vicinity to the point that it does not set. The whole cooking time results in badly overcooked, tough fish.

FISH ROLLS IN CUSTARD
serves 4 to 6

8 small (each about 4 oz/112 g) fillets of haddock
2 teaspoons (10 ml) lemon juice
¼ teaspoon (1.5 g) salt
¼ teaspoon (0.75 g) pepper
1 tablespoon (4 g) finely chopped parsley
1 cup (250 ml) milk
1 egg

Preheat the oven to 350°F. Roll up each fillet, starting with the thinner end if there is one. Fasten each roll with a toothpick. Arrange in a baking dish that holds them snugly. Sprinkle on the lemon juice, salt, and pepper. Beat the egg with the milk and pour around the rolled fillets. Finely chop the parsley and sprinkle evenly over the top. Bake for 35 to 40 minutes, or until the custard (at least around the rim) is set.

---

105 Kiffins (a)

~~War Cake~~
½ lb Butter
½ .. Sugar
a plate of flour
¼ teasp soda
½ teasp cream tartar

Put butter and sugar in a basin
Mix cream of tartar & soda in ½ cup cold water. Throw this over butter & sugar   Put in small quantity of flour & mix into a soft dough, turn out on board. Work in enough flour to make stiff paste, roll out thin and cut in fingers

This recipe was taken directly from the 1905 cookbook (see Chapter 2), where it is spelled kyffins. Even though kyffin is a Welsh noun and proper name, we have no idea why these biscuits are called that.

Although we mixed the tartar and soda together as in the recipe, this is not the ideal procedure, because the two react immediately in the water. Better, in fact, to mix the tartar with the dough, then suspend the soda alone in the water.

These are a pleasant, slightly brittle, not-too-sweet biscuit.

KIFFINS (a)
makes 90 or more biscuits

1 cup (225 g) butter
1¼ cups (250 g) sugar
¼ teaspoon (1.25 g) baking soda
½ teaspoon (2.5 g) cream of tartar

½ cup (125 ml) cold water
3¾ cups (565 g) flour, plus more as needed for rolling

Preheat the oven to 350°F. Lightly grease 2 baking sheets (or use parchment or silicone mats). Cream the butter and sugar together. Stir the tartar and soda into the cold water until suspended, then mix with the butter and sugar. Mix in about 3 cups of the flour or enough to form a stiff dough that can be turned out, then knead in the rest of the flour. When the full amount of flour has been incorporated, halve it for ease of handling, and roll each into a rough rectangle slightly bigger than 8 by 12 inches, using a little extra flour as required to stop it from sticking. Trim the edges to create a neat rectangle 8 by 12 inches, and cut into 8 equal strips lengthways and 4 across the width, to yield 32 pieces. Repeat with the other half, then press the scraps from both halves together and re-roll to yield another 24 to 30 pieces. Place on the prepared baking sheets. Bake 20 to 25 minutes or until the pieces are lightly browned on top.

> 106 Kiffins (b)
>
> 1 cup butter   1 cup sugar ½ cup sour milk
> 1 teasp soda
> Flour to make proper consistency
> to roll thin.

This kiffin recipe is much the same as the first, with slightly less sugar, more baking soda, and sour milk taking the place of the tartar as the acid to make the soda work. Buttermilk, or regular milk with a teaspoon of vinegar added, can replace the sour milk.

KIFFINS (b)
makes 90 or more biscuits

1 cup (225 g) butter
1 cup (200 g) sugar
1 teaspoon (5 g) baking soda

½ cup (125 ml) sour milk or equivalent
3¾ cups (565 g) flour, plus more as needed for rolling

Mix the baking soda with the sugar, and cream this with the butter. Mix in the sour milk, then proceed as in recipe 105.

> ### 107 Chop – Suey
>
> is made with 1 chopped
> onion   3 diced potatoes   ½ lb chopped
> meat 1½ cups tomatoes 2 tablesp
> fat & half cup rice
> Boil rice 10 minutes then add
> Potatoes and cook till soft. Brown onions in the fat, add the meat
> & cook till brown, then add
> rice and potatoes & brown all in a baking dish

Chop suey spread out from New York around 1900 after Chinese cooks popularized the dish by using ingredients familiar to Americans, as in this recipe. By 1920 it had reached most cities in the US, and recipes were frequent in the press, which is likely where Mrs. Ayre got hers, because an essentially identical recipe appeared in the *Evening Telegram*, St. John's, in December 1918. Chop suey seems to have been popular with the general public, because a restaurant of the day, the Blue Puttee, had Chop Suey Sundae on its menu, which presumably had little to do with the savoury meat-and-potatoes version here. Sweet versions of chop suey were made from chopped dried fruits and nuts.

Either Mrs. Ayre was still adding to her recipe collection late in 1918, or she saw the same recipe elsewhere earlier. Fortunately, she—or her cook—spotted the mistake in the published version, where *riced* potatoes should have been *diced* potatoes.

The meat can be raw, or cooked leftovers, but the cooking time will vary depending on which is used.

No doubt this was a bit avant-garde for Newfoundland in its day, the first faint

breath of exotic food, and the version here seems typical of the totally Americanized recipes that were popular at the time.

We were dubious about this recipe, but it tastes better if you think of it as a rather dry, meat and vegetable stew.

CHOP SUEY

serves 4 to 6

½ cup (90 g) uncooked rice
2 cups (500 ml) water
2 tablespoons (30 g) lard or butter
1 medium (about 5 oz/150 g, untrimmed weight) onion
3 medium (about 16 oz/450 g, total untrimmed weight) potatoes
½ pound (225 g) meat
1½ cups (375 g) tomatoes
salt and pepper to taste

Preheat the oven to 350°F. Boil the rice in the water about 10 minutes. Peel and chop the potatoes into ½-inch chunks, add to the rice in the saucepan, and simmer until soft.

Meanwhile, chop the meat into ¼-inch dice and the onion into ½-inch dice. Fry the onions in the fat until translucent and starting to brown, add the diced meat, and continue to fry until it is cooked through (if using cooked leftovers, just heat through). Season to taste. Coarsely chop the tomatoes, add to the frying pan, and heat through. Mix this with the cooked rice and potatoes and season again. Spoon the mixture into a 1½ to 2-quart baking dish or pie dish, and bake 30 to 40 minutes until the top is flecked with brown.

108 Date Cake

1 lb dates   ¾ cup sugar   ½ cup flour
1 teasp baking powder   ½ lb walnuts
3 eggs (separate)

This recipe does not work on two counts. First, the whole point of separating the eggs is so that whipped whites can lighten the mixture. But the mixture is too stiff to fold in the whites, so we have added milk in our recipe below. Second, there are too many dates and nuts for the fabric of the cake to support. It will work with any amount around 50 per cent or less than those given. In our recipe we used 25 per cent of the amounts in the recipe.

DATE CAKE
makes one 8-inch (20 cm) cake

¾ cup (150 g) sugar
3 eggs
½ cup (75 g) flour
1 teaspoon (5 g) baking powder

¼ cup (65 ml) milk
½ cup (56 g) pecans or walnuts
1 cup (110 g) dates

Preheat the oven to 350°F. Grease and flour an 8-inch cake pan. Chop the dates and nuts coarsely.

Separate the eggs. Beat the sugar and yolks together. Mix the flour and baking powder, then beat them in alternately with the milk. Stir in the chopped nuts and dates, breaking up any clumps.

Whip the whites to stiff peaks, and fold into the mixture. Scrape and pour into the prepared cake pan and bake 35 to 40 minutes, or until a small skewer inserted in the thickest part comes out clean. Turn out on a rack to cool.

109 Spice Cake

½ cup butter   1½ sugar
3 eggs   ½ cup milk   2 teasp c. of tartar
1 teasp soda   ½ cup currants
1 cup raisins   1 cloves   1 cinnamon
1 nutmeg   3 cups flour
Beat eggs & sugar   add milk & melted butter add flour   into stiff dough

....

1 cup sugar   1 cup raisins   ½ butter
1 egg ½ teasp soda   2 tablesp sour milk
1½ cups flour   ½ teasp spice

In the original notebook, the dotted line above is a page break, so what at first sight looks like a continuous recipe written over two pages is in fact two recipes under the same name and number. We have called them the first and second spice cake.

The first spice cake

This is a voluminous cake, so if an 8-inch cake pan is used, use a deep one, or use a regular-depth 9-inch pan. There is nothing magical about adding melted butter as opposed to the more usual technique of creaming the butter and sugar: both are designed to achieve an even dispersion of the butter in the mixture. If you use melted butter, let it cool before adding (there is a risk of very hot butter cooking some of the egg), but use it while it is still liquid.

If you prefer a stronger spice taste, you will favour this cake over the second. But overall, the two are similar.

SPICE CAKE (first cake)
makes one 8 or 9-inch (20 or 23 cm) cake

1½ cups (300 g) sugar
3 eggs
½ cup (110 g) butter
1 teaspoon (3 g) cloves
1 teaspoon (3 g) cinnamon
1 teaspoon (3 g) nutmeg

3 cups (450 g) flour
2 teaspoons (10 g) cream of tartar
1 teaspoon (5 g) baking soda
½ cup (125 ml) milk
½ cup (75 g) currants
1 cup (150 g) raisins

Preheat the oven to 350°F. Grease and flour a cake pan. Melt the butter and let it cool. Beat the eggs and sugar together, then beat in the cooled liquid butter. Beat in the spices. Mix the flour, baking soda, and tartar together, and combine with the egg-butter mixture alternating with the milk. Mix in the currants and raisins. Scrape the batter into the prepared cake pan, roughly smoothing the top. Bake 65 to 75 minutes, or until the top is richly browned and a small skewer inserted in the thickest part comes out clean.

The second spice cake

Sour milk is called for here. But in the 21st century milk does not go sour as it did in the early 20th century. Most of it has been ultra-pasteurized, so it ferments rather unpleasantly rather than going gracefully sour. So unless you are lucky enough to have raw milk, don't use milk that has just gone off in the refrigerator—use one of the substitutes mentioned below.

The 2 tablespoons of sour milk are not enough; it needs ½ cup. Use buttermilk, or regular milk with 1 teaspoon of vinegar stirred in, to replace the sour milk. Equal parts of nutmeg, cinnamon, and cloves were used to make up the ½ teaspoon of mixed spice.

This is the better of these two spice cakes.

SPICE CAKE (second cake)
makes one 8-inch (20 cm) cake

1 cup (200 g) sugar
½ cup (110 g) butter
1 egg
½ teaspoon (2.5 g) baking soda

½ cup (125 ml) sour milk or equivalent
1½ cups (225 g) flour
½ teaspoon (1.5 g) mixed spices
1 cup (150 g) raisins

Preheat the oven to 350°F. Grease and flour an 8-inch cake pan. Cream the butter and sugar together. Beat in the egg and spices. Mix the flour and baking soda, and mix this in, alternating with the milk. Stir in the raisins, and scrape this into the prepared pan, roughly smoothing the top. Bake 50 to 60 minutes, or until the top is richly browned and a small skewer inserted in the thickest part comes out clean.

110 Rice Cake

1 cup flour   1½ cups rice
6 oz butter   6 oz sugar   1 teasp soda
2 teasp cinnamon   1 nutmeg
½ pt milk   ½ lb chopped raisins or citron
Bake 1½ hours in rather slow oven

Note that the rice is cooked rice; that much raw rice would be totally out of proportion. This is a good way of using leftovers. This cake could rightly be called a spice cake. The rice gives it an unusual texture, but it is overall a pleasant cake.

RICE CAKE
makes one 8-inch (20 cm) cake

6 ounces (170 g) butter
6 ounces (170 g) sugar
2 teaspoons (6 g) cinnamon
1 teaspoon (3 g) nutmeg
1 cup (150 g) flour

1 teaspoon (5 g) baking soda
1½ cups (180 g) cooked rice
1 cup (250 ml) milk
1½ cups (225 g) raisins

Preheat the oven to 325°F. Grease and flour an 8-inch cake pan. Cream together the butter and sugar. Mix in the spices. Mix the flour with the baking soda. Add the rice, flour, and milk alternately to the butter and sugar to make a loose batter. Mix in the raisins. Scrape into the prepared pan and bake about 75 minutes, or until a small skewer inserted into the thickest part comes out clean. Turn out on a rack to cool.

111 Potato Scones

1 cup mashed potato   1 cup corn meal cooked in 2 cups boiling water
2 tablesp shortening   1 teasp salt
1 cup barley flour   4 teasp baking powder or 3 teasp & 1 egg

This recipe needs some liquid because without it the dough is impossibly dry and crumbly. It is better with 3 teaspoons of baking powder plus 1 egg, rather than just 4 teaspoons of baking powder, but if you opt for the latter combination, add an extra 3 tablespoons of milk.

We are not convinced of the virtues of barley flour—this recipe works fine with regular flour.

POTATO SCONES
makes about 12 scones

2 cups (500 ml) water
1 cup (160 g) cornmeal
1 cup (200 g) mashed potato
2 tablespoons (30 g) shortening or butter
1 teaspoon (6.5 g) salt
1 cup (150 g) barley flour
3 teaspoons (15 g) baking powder
½ cup (125 ml) milk
1 egg

Preheat the oven to 400°F. Lightly grease a baking sheet (or use parchment or a silicone mat). Bring the water to a boil, pour in the cornmeal while stirring constantly, and simmer for 1 or 2 minutes or until the cornmeal is a thick, stiff mass. Remove from the heat, and mash in the potato, shortening, and salt.

Mix the barley flour with the baking powder and mix them with the cornmeal-potato mixture. Turn out onto a lightly floured surface and knead briefly to make sure everything is well combined. Press out (or use a rolling pin) to about 1 inch thick. Cut out disks with a 2½-inch cookie cutter. The dough is quite sticky, so wipe the cutter between each disk. Lay the disks on the prepared baking sheet. Press the scraps together and cut out more disks to make about 12 in total. Bake about 35 minutes, or until the tops are fissured and lightly browned. Cool on racks.

---

112 Ginger Snaps.

1 cup shortening   1 cup molasses   ½ cup corn or maple syrup   ½ cup sugar   1 egg beaten light   1½ cups corn flour   1 tablesp ginger   ½ teasp salt   1 teasp soda

---

The recipe makes a lot of gingersnaps; half a batch may be more convenient.

The batter flows and spreads as it bakes, so the cookies have to be spaced out. Using the amounts recommended below, put them about 5 inches apart, centre-to-centre. A convenient arrangement is 8 portions of batter on a 12 by 16-inch baking sheet arranged in a double quincunx. If the baking sheet is buckled, the batter will flow downhill as it bakes and fuse with its neighbour, so try to use a flat, level sheet.

Do not try to lift them from the baking sheet straight from of the oven: they will crumple. Let them cool until still pliable but firm enough to be picked up on a thin, metal spatula.

Makes a good, thin, brittle gingersnap.

GINGER SNAPS
makes about 100 snaps, about 3½ inches (9 cm) in diameter

- 1 cup (195 g) shortening
- 1 cup (250 ml) molasses
- ½ cup (125 ml) corn syrup or maple syrup
- 1 egg
- 1 tablespoon (5 g) ginger
- ½ teaspoon (3.3 g) salt
- 1½ cups (180 g) corn flour
- 1 teaspoon (5 g) baking soda

Preheat the oven to 350°F. Lightly grease (or use parchment or a silicone mat) at least 2 baking sheets. Mix the shortening, molasses, and syrup, followed by the egg, ginger, and salt. Mix the baking soda with the corn flour and beat this into the mixture to make a batter.

Drop about 2 teaspoons of batter for each cookie, well spaced out, on the baking sheet. Bake 8 to 9 minutes, or until the batter has completely flattened out and the surface is evenly wrinkled. Remove from the oven and let cool 3 or 4 minutes, then lift the snaps onto a rack to continue cooling.

113 Tomato Jelly

Cook 2 cups tomatoes with 1 slice onion
1 teasp salt little pepper for 20 minutes
Strain through sieve. Then add
2 tablesp gelatine previously dissolved
1 cup cold water

Rubbing the tomato-onion mixture through a sieve is historically correct but tediously hard work, so by all means cheat a little and use a blender.

Presumably this was intended as a savoury accompaniment to meat and vegetables, to be used like a relish on the side. It is pleasant but undistinguished.

TOMATO JELLY
makes about 3 cups (750 ml)

2 cups (500 g) canned tomatoes
1 thick slice (50 g) of a large onion, or 1 very small onion
1 teaspoon (6.5 g) salt
½ teaspoon (1.5 g) pepper
2 tablespoons (20 g) granulated gelatine
1 cup (250 ml) cold water

Chop the tomatoes and onion coarsely. Place in a small saucepan with the salt and pepper, bring to a boil, and simmer on a low heat about 20 minutes, or until the onions are very soft.

Meanwhile, sprinkle the gelatine over the water in a wide bowl and leave to soak.

When the onions are completely cooked, rub the tomato-onion mixture through a coarse sieve (or blend), and return to the saucepan. Add the soaked gelatine with all the water and bring back to a boil, stirring frequently. Pour into a 1-quart mould or other similar container and leave to cool and set.

114 Molasses Pie

1 cup molasses ½ cup white
sugar juice of 2 lemons or vinegar
3 tablesp moistened smoothed flour
2 tablesp melted butter
1 teasp nutmeg   1 teasp cinnamon
Mix well all beaten yolks of
2 eggs then [?] stiff whites
mix   bake in [p]astry shells about
25 minutes

This is much better with lemon juice rather than vinegar offsetting the sweet molasses.

The whipped egg whites are a puzzle because the mixture is too fluid to fold them in, so we assumed that "mix" means simply stirring them in—which defeats the purpose of whipping them in the first place. We tried this recipe with the eggs not separated but simply whisked in, and it does not seem to make much difference.

Be careful when filling the pastry shell. Depending on the exact dimensions of the shell, there may be too much filling.

MOLASSES PIE
makes one 9-inch (23 cm) open-faced pie or more smaller pies

1 pre-baked 9-inch (23 cm) pastry shell, or more smaller shells
3 tablespoons (30 g) flour
2 tablespoons (30 ml) water
2 eggs
1 cup (250 ml) molasses
½ cup (100 g) sugar
½ cup (125 ml) lemon juice (from about 2 lemons), or ½ cup vinegar
2 tablespoons (30 g) melted butter
1 teaspoon (3 g) nutmeg
1 teaspoon (3 g) cinnamon

Ahead of time, make and bake a 9-inch pastry shell. Preheat the oven to 350°F. Gradually mash the flour with the water to make a smooth, lump-free paste. Separate the eggs. Mix the flour paste, molasses, sugar, lemon juice (or vinegar), melted butter, nutmeg, cinnamon, and egg yolks. Whisk the egg whites to stiff peaks and stir them in until evenly distributed.

Pour all the mixture—or as much of it as will fit—into the pre-baked pastry shell (or shells). Bake 55 to 65 minutes (less for smaller pies), or until the mixture just wobbles when the pie plate is nudged. Cool.

115 Chocolate Cream

dissolve ¼ cake chocolate in little hot milk   Have a pint milk heating in double boiler & add dissolved chocolate ½ cup sugar   yolks 2 eggs 3 tablesp corn-flour. Stir until thick   meringue of whites when done place on top

The immediate question is, what was one-quarter cake of chocolate? If the chocolate came in slabs weighing either ½ pound or 1 pound (a reasonable guess), then the amount called for here was 2 or 4 ounces. We tried this recipe with both amounts, and both work fine. Our recipe uses the lesser amount. Which chocolate to use is a matter of personal preference, but if unsweetened chocolate is used, add an extra 2 tablespoons of sugar.

The meringue topping has a much better texture and remains stable for longer if some sugar is whipped with the whites, as below.

CHOCOLATE CREAM
serves 4 to 6

2 squares (60 g) chocolate
2 tablespoons (30 ml) milk
2 cups (500 ml) milk

½ cup (100 g) sugar
2 egg yolks
3 tablespoons (45 ml) corn flour

For the meringue
2 egg whites   ¼ cup (50 g) sugar

Gently warm the chocolate with the 2 tablespoons of milk in a small bowl and stir until the chocolate is all melted.

Separate the eggs. Heat the 2 cups of milk and ½ cup of sugar in a bowl over simmering water. Whisk in the corn flour, egg yolks, and melted chocolate. Continue to heat over the simmering water, whisking frequently, until the mixture has thickened and feels like a loose jelly. Pour into a 1-quart serving dish and let cool.

Whip the egg whites to soft peaks, then add the sugar in portions and whip to stiff peaks. Spread this meringue evenly over the top of the cooled chocolate cream.

116 Moll's Cake

2 eggs (separate)
¾ cup sugar
1 tablesp ordinary flour fill up
with ¾ potato flour
1 teasp baking powder
Put sugar in whites
Sift flour. Use silver knife to stir
Bake in quick oven 6 minutes
4 minutes to rise. Hot oven

Whites & sugar and beat. Add yolks
Beat 5 minutes.

This recipe looks simple but closer inspection reveals a minefield of ambiguity. We understand the instruction about using a silver knife—in the days before stainless steel many utensils were made of carbon steel that would discolour and taint many foods.

But the rest of it is problematic in the extreme. We have tried many different combinations of the ingredients, and wasted several dozen eggs, all with equally poor results.

So we confess we are defeated by this one; it seems essentially indecipherable. The recipe is so sketchy it may have been written from memorized verbatim instructions. Of course, by radically altering the ingredients and method a cake can be created, but such a cake is so far removed from the original that it is essentially a new recipe, which is not the intent here.

We tried many permutations, and the following is where we left this recipe.

MOLL'S CAKE
makes one 8-inch (20 cm) cake

2 eggs
¾ cup (150 g) sugar
1 tablespoon (10 g) flour
¾ tablespoon (7.5 g) potato flour
1 teaspoon (5 g) baking powder

Preheat the oven to 400°F. Grease and flour an 8-inch cake pan. Separate the eggs. Whip the whites to soft peaks, then add the sugar in portions while continuing to whip to stiff peaks. Beat in the yolks. Mix both flours with the baking powder, and fold in. Pour and scrape into the prepared pan and bake about 20 minutes, or until a small skewer inserted in the thickest part comes out clean. Turn out on a rack to cool.

117 Carrie's Chocolate Cake

Put ½ cup butter and about ¾ cup sugar
in a bowl and cream
Beat 3 eggs until very light. Beat
All together until fluffy. Beat do not stir.
Put chocolate (size of 2 walnuts)
Cut up in sm pieces in cup. Half fill
cup with boiling water. Let boil 2 or 3
minutes, then fill cup with milk.
Throw in bowl where eggs were and
let cool a little
Add to mixture and 1½ cups flour –
not too full
2 big teaspoons baking powder
Pinch salt, vanilla, beat very spongy
Put warm in oven. Bake in very hot oven

Icing.   Cut up not quite 2 walnuts
chocolate. Add lg lump butter - nearly
tablespoon.   Add vanilla pinch salt
Put all in bowl.
Put 1½ cups sugar to boil with ¾ cup milk
Boil until strings. Pour on choc & beat

In many parts of America, walnuts were common, so were frequently used as baking measurements in the 19th and early 20th century, and we suspect that is where this recipe came from. But many people now have no idea of the size of a walnut, and, in any case, it is a woefully imprecise measure. Here we take a walnut to be 1 ounce.

The method of melting chocolate with boiling water or syrup is not widely practiced, but it works.

CARRIE'S CHOCOLATE CAKE
makes one 8-inch (20 cm) cake

½ cup (110 g) butter
¾ cup (150 g) sugar
3 eggs
pinch (0.1 g) salt
½ teaspoon (2.5 ml) vanilla

2 squares (60 g) chocolate
boiling water
about ½ cup (125 ml) milk
1½ cups (225 g) flour
4 teaspoons (20 g) baking powder

For the icing

1½ cups (300 g) sugar
¾ cup (190 ml) milk
2 squares (60 g) chocolate

1 tablespoon (15 g) butter
¼ teaspoon (1 ml) vanilla
pinch (0.1 g) salt

Preheat the oven to 425°F. Grease and flour an 8-inch cake pan. Cream the butter and sugar together. Beat the eggs until very pale, then beat into the butter-sugar mixture. Beat in the salt and vanilla.

Chop the chocolate coarsely and put into a cup measure. Pour boiling water over the chocolate to about half fill the measuring cup, and stir well. When the chocolate has melted, fill up the measuring cup with milk, stir well, and add this to the butter-sugar-egg mixture.

Mix the flour and baking powder, then beat this into the mixture. Pour and scrape the batter into the prepared pan, and bake 30 to 35 minutes, or until a small skewer inserted into the thickest part comes out clean. Turn out on a rack to cool.

When the cake is cool, make the icing. Coarsely chop the chocolate and put it in a wide bowl with the butter, vanilla, and salt. Boil the sugar with the milk for about 10 to 12 minutes to the thread stage. Immediately pour slowly onto the chocolate, stirring constantly to help the chocolate melt and dissolve in the syrup. Set aside to cool. When the icing gets quite thick and barely flows off a spoon (about 60 minutes or more), pour a small portion on top of the cake. If it flows rapidly toward the edge, let the rest of the icing cool some more, until another portion flows reluctantly. Pour the icing evenly over the top, and either let it flow down the sides, or spread it over the sides with a spatula.

118 Nut Cinnamon Cake

1 table sp cinnamon
1 cup flour
1 teaspoon baking powder
sift over ¾ cup chopped walnuts

½ cup butter }   cream
1 cup sugar   }
add 2 egg yolks mixed with ½ cup milk

add flour etc then beaten whites

Icing –
½ cup butter   1 teasp vanilla
½ cup milk
2 cups brown sugar
boil until forms soft ball   –   Beat.
(Milk or butter will soften if too stiff)

Makes a pleasant cake, although the cinnamon was overdone. Unless you are very sure of the freshness of the walnuts, it is best to use pecans.

The icing is very similar to the chocolate icing of the previous recipe, where the advice was to boil it to the thread stage. In this one the soft-ball stage is recommended. But either temperature works in both cases.

NUT CINNAMON CAKE
makes one 8-inch (20 cm) cake

1 cup (150 g) flour
1 tablespoon (9 g) cinnamon
   (or less to taste)
1 teaspoon (5 g) baking powder
¾ cup (75 g) walnuts

½ cup (110 g) butter
1 cup (200 g) sugar
2 eggs
½ cup (125 ml) milk

For the icing

½ cup (110 g) butter
1 teaspoon (5 ml) vanilla

½ cup (125 ml) milk
2 cups (300 g) brown sugar

Preheat the oven to 350°F. Grease and flour an 8-inch cake pan. Chop the nuts coarsely. Mix the flour, cinnamon, and baking powder, then mix this with the nuts.

Separate the eggs. Cream the butter and sugar, then mix in the yolks and milk. Combine this mixture with the flour-nut mixture. Whip the whites to stiff peaks and fold into the mixture. Scrape into the prepared pan and bake 30 to 35 minutes, or until a small skewer inserted into the thickest part comes out clean. Turn out on a rack to cool.

Icing

Mix all the ingredients in a small saucepan and bring to a boil. Simmer it to the soft-ball stage. Cool, stirring occasionally. When the icing gets quite thick and barely flows off a spoon (about 60 minutes or more), pour a small portion on top of the cake. If it flows rapidly toward the edge, let the rest of the icing cool some more, until another portion flows reluctantly. Then pour on all the icing evenly over the top, and either let it flow down the sides or spread it over the sides with a spatula.

119 Apple Jelly (marmalade)

Pare core & quarter & slice enough apples to make 4 lbs. Slice 3 lemons very thinly Add to the apples with 1 qt water Cook until apple is soft. Press through colander and add an equal amount of sugar and 1½ cups of blanched almonds. Stir & cook until thick like jelly about 15 minutes.

To end up with the specified 4 pounds of trimmed weight apple you need to start with about 18 whole medium apples, each about 5 ounces, a total weight of about 6 pounds, but have a few extra on hand in case there is a bad one in the batch. Which variety to use is a matter of personal choice; we used Granny Smiths.

Pressing through a colander is a good but laborious way of mashing up the apples and lemons—the latter in particular need reducing to uniform pieces; the apples mush themselves up during cooking. But a food mill, or pulsing in a food processor, mashes them much more quickly and with minimal hard labour.

The blanched almonds can be either slivered or chopped, but whole ones are too big.

As the name suggests, this is much more a marmalade than a jelly, but it is not a great example of the genre. This recipe fills about seven 2-cup Mason jars to the neck.

APPLE JELLY (MARMALADE)
makes about 12 cups (3 l)

4 pounds (1.8 kg, trimmed weight) apples
3 lemons
1 quart (1 l) water
about 9 cups (1800 g) sugar
1½ cups (150 g) blanched almonds

Slice the ends off the lemons, then cut into quarters lengthways. Cut out the centre line of pith, which reveals the ends of the pits—remove with the point of a small knife. Sliver the de-pitted quarters of lemon thinly, and put them and any juice with the water into a 6-quart saucepan. Peel, core, and quarter the apples until you have the required amount. Slice the quarters roughly and put in the saucepan with the lemon. Bring to a boil and simmer until the lemon slices are soft and the apple well cooked and mushy. Push this through a colander (or use a food mill or processor) and measure the volume of the result. Put it all back in the saucepan with an equal volume of sugar. Add the almonds and bring back to a boil. Simmer until thickened to your liking, or to the setting point of 220°F. Ladle into clean Mason jars.

120 Raisin Bread

3 cups Graham flour
5 teasp baking powder
1½ salt
¼ cup sugar
1½ milk and water
1 cup raisins floured
Mix dry ingredients add milk & Raisins. Put in greased pan & allow to stand 30 minutes in a warm place   Bake 45 mins in mod oven

By all means use graham flour, but whole wheat flour works just as well and is easier to find.

Flouring the raisins is not necessary here, but it helps you see any clumps of raisins that need separating; elsewhere this technique is supposed to stop them sinking in a more fluid batter.

The recipe works with any proportions of milk and water; here we use equal proportions of milk and water.

There's no reason to let the dough stand for 30 minutes before putting in the oven. In a yeast-risen loaf, that would be a crucial rising time, but baking powder does not work the same way. Maybe it allows the flour time to absorb more liquid and make a stiffer dough? We have tried this both with and without that 30-minute rise, and it makes no difference.

RAISIN BREAD
makes 1 loaf

3 cups (450 g) graham or whole wheat flour
5 teaspoons (25 g) baking powder
1½ teaspoons (10 g) salt
¼ cup (50 g) sugar
1½ cups (375 ml) milk and water
1 cup (150 g) raisins
1 tablespoon (10 g) flour

Preheat the oven to 350°F. Grease a loaf pan, about 5 by 10 inches. Toss the raisins with the 1 tablespoon of flour and break up any clumps.

Mix together the flour, baking powder, salt, and sugar. Stir in the milk and water to make a soft and sticky dough, then stir in the raisins.

Turn the dough out onto a counter and fold it over a few times to evenly distribute the raisins. Form the dough into a rough rectangle about the same shape as the loaf pan. Lift the dough, drop it into the pan, push it out to fill the pan, then smooth off the top with wet fingers.

Let stand 30 minutes in a warm place (optional). Then bake 45 to 55 minutes, or until the loaf is brown at the edges and starting to pull away from the pan. Turn out onto a rack to cool.

Evening Telegram, December 28, 1895.

121 Jelly.

2 cups brown sugar
½ cup hot water
Boil 10 minutes
1 pk Knox gelatine
Soak in 1½ cups cold water 10 mins
When syrup is cooked pour gradually over soaked gelatine let cool then whip whites of 2 eggs very stiff.
Pour the cooled jelly over whites with 1 cup nuts chopped fine.
Make custard of the whites & serve with snaps.

We hope Mrs. Ayre (or her cook) spotted the mistake: the custard, of course, is made with the egg yolks, not the whites. There is no need to use hot water for mixing with the sugar since it is all going to be boiled, so start with cold water. In 10 minutes of simmering, the temperature of the sugar solution gets to about the thread stage, which is hot enough to dissolve the gelatine when mixed together.

As elsewhere, we used pecans, although presumably any nuts can be used.

Mrs. Ayre's directions for combining the jelly, egg whites, and nuts are ambiguous. The method below worked for us.

This is not an inspiring jelly. It is too sweet, lacks any compensatory acidity, and the nuts add nothing except unexpected and unwelcome texture.

JELLY
serves 4 to 6

1 tablespoon (10 g) granulated gelatine
1½ cups (375 ml) cold water
2 cups (300 g) brown sugar
½ cup (125 ml) water
2 eggs
1 cup (100 g) nuts

Sprinkle the gelatine over the larger amount of water in a wide bowl and leave it to soak while the sugar simmers. Bring the sugar and the smaller amount of water to a boil and simmer for 10 minutes. Pour the hot sugar syrup over the soaked gelatine, stirring to dissolve it. Set aside to cool, then chill.

When the mixture has set to a loose jelly, chop the nuts to pieces no bigger than ¼ inch, and stir these into the jelly, breaking up the jelly as you do so. Separate the eggs. Whip the egg whites to stiff peaks and fold into the nut-jelly mixture. If desired, make a custard with the yolks (recipe 55).

122 Apple Charlotte

6 lg apples ½ box gelatine 1 pt cream sugar to taste. Pare and steam apples until tender then press through a colander add sugar. Soak gelatine half an hr then add to hot apples. Stir until dissolved Pour into basin stand in ice water and beat until mixture begins to thicken. Then add cream whipped Put away to harden

The recipe calls for steaming the apples, a way of cooking the apples without adding any water. If you do not have a steamer, improvise by hanging a colander in the top of a saucepan that just matches its size, and laying the lid on top.

Pushing the cooked apples through a colander is effective but laborious; food mills or potato mashers involve much less work for the same result.

The amount of sugar needed depends on the sweetness of the apples. We used Granny Smiths, so the sugar in our recipe reflects their tart nature. For a sweeter apple, reduce the sugar slightly.

We have translated the half box of gelatine in our recipe below. There is no need to soak granular gelatine for 30 minutes. But it is essential to make sure that it is totally dissolved, so stir in the sugar and soaked gelatine while the apples are still hot. If granules of undissolved gelatine remain after a thorough stirring, heat gently for 5 or more minutes to make sure it is all dissolved.

Standing the mixture in ice water speeds up the cooling, but it is not necessary. If the mixture is over-cooled and it sets, gently warm to loosen it.

APPLE CHARLOTTE
serves 4 to 6

2 tablespoons (20 g) granular gelatine
½ cup (125 ml) water
6 large (about 225 g each, untrimmed) apples
2 cups (500 ml) cream
1 cup (200 g) sugar

Sprinkle the gelatine over the water in a wide, shallow bowl and soak for at least 5 minutes. Peel, core, and slice the apples, and place in a steamer. Have a kettle of boiling water on standby to replenish the water in the steamer if necessary. Steam the apples until completely soft. Push them through a colander or mash. While the apples are still hot, stir in the sugar and soaked gelatine. Warm the mixture if necessary to dissolve all the gelatine. Cool. When the apple mixture is getting very thick (but before it sets), whip the cream to soft peaks and fold in. Scrape into a 2-quart serving bowl and cool until set.

123 Devils food cake

¼ cup butter beaten until creamy
1 cup sugar added gradually
two squares of unsweetened chocolate melted.   2 eggs well beaten
½ cup milk
1 ⅓ cups of flour mixed with
3 teasp baking pdr.
½ "   salt
1 "   vanilla
Bake 45 mins in mod oven

Melt the chocolate by any method, but one of the easiest is to put it in a small bowl over barely simmering water. Despite the catchy title, this is not a particularly distinguished chocolate cake.

DEVILS FOOD CAKE
makes one 8-inch (20 cm) cake

2 squares (60 g) unsweetened chocolate
¼ cup (55 g) butter
1 cup (200 g) sugar
2 eggs
½ teaspoon (3.3 g) salt

1 teaspoon (5 ml) vanilla
1 ⅓ cups (200 g) flour
3 teaspoons (15 g) baking powder
½ cup (125 ml) milk

Preheat the oven to 350°F. Grease and flour an 8-inch cake pan.
Melt the chocolate. Cream the butter and sugar together. Beat in the melted chocolate. Beat in the eggs, salt, and vanilla. Mix the flour with the baking powder, and mix this into the chocolate mixture, alternating with the milk. Scrape the batter into the prepared pan

and bake 35 to 40 minutes, or until a small skewer inserted in the thickest part comes out clean. Turn out on a rack to cool.

124 Light Fruit Cake

1 lb flour
½ " sugar
3 oz cherries
½ spoonful soda
3 eggs   &   ½ cup sour milk
½ lb sultanas
4 oz candied peel
2 teasp baking pdr
½ lb butter

If you have no sour milk, use buttermilk; if you have neither, use plain milk—there is enough acidity in the baking powder to activate the soda as well. Because there are relatively few cherries, it best to cut them in half, or leave them whole if desired.

This is an excellent example of a light fruit cake.

LIGHT FRUIT CAKE
makes one 9-inch (23 cm) cake

1 cup (225 g) butter
2 cups + 2 tablespoons (225 g) sugar
3 eggs
3 cups (450 g) flour
2 teaspoons (10 g) baking powder
½ teaspoon (2.5 g) baking soda

½ cup (125 ml) sour milk
1½ cups (225 g) sultanas
¾ cup (85 g) candied cherries
   (about 20 cherries)
1 cup (110 g) candied peel

Preheat the oven to 350°F. Grease and flour a 9-inch cake pan. Cream the sugar and butter together, then mix in the eggs. Mix the flour with the baking powder and baking soda, and mix this in, alternating with the milk. Stir in the sultanas, cherries, and peel.

Scrape the batter into the prepared pan and bake 60 to 65 minutes, or until a small skewer inserted in the thickest part comes out clean. Turn out on a rack to cool.

> ## 125 Angel Cake
>
> pinch salt sifted 5 times
> 1 cup sugar   1 cup milk brought
> 1 "   flour   to boiling point
> 3 teasp baking powder
>
> then add dry ingredients whites
> of 2 eggs beaten stiff & folded in last
> bake in mod oven.

Sifting is unnecessary as long as the dry ingredients are well mixed.

Do not actually boil the milk, because it will froth up and boil over. Just scald it: heat it to the point where it is just fizzing around the edges. After pouring the hot milk into the mixture, work quickly because the heat and moisture will start the baking powder working before it goes in the oven.

This is a pleasant but undistinguished white cake.

ANGEL CAKE
makes one 8-inch (20 cm) cake

1 cup (200 g) sugar   pinch (0.1 g) of salt
1 cup (150 g) flour   1 cup (250 ml) milk
3 teaspoons (15 g) baking powder   2 egg whites

Preheat the oven to 350°F. Grease and flour an 8-inch cake pan.

Mix the sugar, flour, baking powder, and salt. Scald the milk and pour it over the dry ingredients, stirring as you do. Whip the egg whites to stiff peaks and fold into the mixture. Pour and scrape into the prepared pan and bake 30 to 35 minutes, or until a small skewer inserted in the thickest part comes out clean. Turn out on a rack to cool.

> ### 126 Delicate White Cake (Eaten Stale)
>
> cream together 2 cups sugar & ½ cup butter
> Add alternately 3 cups flour which have
> been sifted with 3 sm teasp. baking powder
> & 1 cup sweet milk begin with flour
> in alternating these two ingredients
> and beat well after each addition for
> the more beaten this stage finer - grain
> Last fold in stiffly-beaten whites of
> 4 eggs and add ½ teasp lemon extract
> Pour in pan and bake 40 mins mod. oven
> (Crème – menthe – on icing)

This cake is no better for being eaten stale, but the absence of egg yolks means that it goes stale more slowly than others, so perhaps that is the intent.

The single cup of milk specified by Mrs. Ayre creates a batter so stiff that it is impossible to fold in the whipped whites, so we increased the amount of milk. But even then it helps to first mix in a little of the whipped whites to make folding in the rest easier.

DELICATE WHITE CAKE (EATEN STALE)
makes one 8-inch (20 cm) cake

- 2 cups (400 g) sugar
- ½ cup (110 g) butter
- ½ teaspoon (2.5 ml) lemon essence
- 3 cups (450 g) flour
- 3 teaspoons (15 g) baking powder
- 1¼ cups (315 ml) milk
- 4 egg whites

Preheat the oven to 350°F. Grease and flour a 3-inch-deep, 8-inch cake pan.

Cream together the sugar and butter. Stir in the lemon essence. Mix the flour and baking powder, and stir this alternately with the milk into the butter-sugar mixture. Whip the egg whites to stiff peaks, and mix about ½ cup of them with the batter to loosen it, then fold in the remainder of the whites. Scrape into the prepared pan and bake for about 75 minutes, or until a small skewer inserted in the thickest part comes out clean. Turn out on a rack to cool.

127 Finger - Rolls.

Heat 2 cups of sweet milk until tepid. Take ¼ cup of this tepid milk & dissolve in it 1 compressed yeast cake Then add the dissolved yeast to the remainder of the milk in a mixing bowl. Add also ¼ cup sugar 1 teasp salt 2 tablesp butter & when it cools slightly 2 well-beaten eggs. Stir well then add 2 cups flour to make a light dough let this rise till spongy, then beat in 4 more cups of flour, knead well, and let rise again - but this time until double in bulk (about 3¼ hrs) now cut down the dough & shape into finger rolls, place these rolls in pans to rise again, then when not quite double in bulk, bake for about twenty minutes in a hot oven.

Called finger rolls because they are elongate rather than spherical—the modern hot-dog roll is an exaggerated finger roll. This recipe makes a good bread roll, with the eggs improving the texture.

Make sure the butter is soft before adding it so that it will get dispersed by the kneading. If the butter is hard, melt it and let it cool before adding.

Unless your kitchen is cool, the 3¼ hours to rise the dough the second time is unnecessarily long. It usually needs around half that or no more than 2 hours at a typical room temperature of 72° to 74°F.

Dividing the dough is best done by weight, although an experienced eye can come close. Getting the dough into long sausages is trickier than it looks, because the dough is very elastic and springs back as it is stretched (you will soon appreciate why most bread rolls are globes or ellipses).

FINGER ROLLS
makes about 16 rolls

2 cups (500 ml) milk
¼ cup (50 g) sugar
1 teaspoon (6.5 g) salt
1½ tablespoons (16 g) dry, granular yeast

2 eggs
2 tablespoons (30 g) butter
6 cups (900 g) flour

Warm the milk until tepid (about body temperature), put it in a large 6-quart bowl, stir in the sugar and salt until all dissolved, sprinkle the dry yeast over the surface, and leave it for about 15 minutes, or until small bubbles are visible. Whisk the eggs and stir them in. Stir in about 2 cups flour. Leave about an hour or until the mixture is puffed up and bubbling. Stir in the butter and up to about 3 cups of flour until it gets too stiff to stir, then turn the dough out on a lightly floured surface and knead the dough for about 10 minutes, adding small portions of the remaining flour as needed to prevent the dough from sticking. You may not use all the flour—we had about ⅓ cup left over. Put the dough in a lightly greased, 6-quart bowl, cover with plastic film, and leave it to rise for about 1½ to 2 hours, or until at least doubled in bulk.

Preheat the oven to 400°F. Lightly grease 2 baking sheets, or use parchment or silicone mats. Punch down the dough and divide into 16 portions, or as many as desired. Tuck the ragged edges of each portion underneath, then roll and stretch them out to at least 3 times longer than wide. Place these on the prepared baking sheets, cover with plastic film, and let rise about 30 minutes until about doubled in bulk. Bake about 20 minutes, or until well browned, then turn out on racks to cool.

128 Almond Macaroons

Beat 2 eggs slightly and add 1 cup brown sugar then ½ cup flour mixed & sifted with ½ teasp baking powder and ¼ teaspoon salt. Add 1 cup blanched almonds cut in small pieces. Bake in buttered tins in moderate oven 15 mins.

Brown sugar has an irritating tendency to have little rock-hard lumps in it; remove any you find. We used pre-sliced, blanched almonds, which need no further cutting.

We used standard muffin pans, each cup about 3 inches wide at the top, and 1¼ inches deep. It is not enough to just butter the baking pans, as the recipe indicates—they need both butter and flour to prevent the macaroons from sticking, even for non-stick pans.

ALMOND MACAROONS
makes 12 macaroons

2 eggs
1 cup (150 g) brown sugar
¼ teaspoon (1.5 g) salt

½ cup (75 g) flour
½ teaspoon (2.5 g) baking powder
1 cup (100 g) slivered almonds

Preheat the oven to 350°F. Grease and flour 12 standard muffin cups. Whisk the eggs, salt, and sugar together until the sugar is dissolved and there is no crunch of crystals under the whisk. Mix the flour and baking powder and stir them into the egg mixture. Mix in the slivered almonds. Divide the mixture between the 12 muffin cups, filling them about one-third full. Bake 15 to 20 minutes, or until the macaroons have risen more or less to the rim of the cups and their tops are well browned. Turn out on a rack to cool.

129 Raisin Biscuits

1 cup raisins chopped   ⅓ cup milk
2 cups flour   2 teasp baking powder
½ teasp salt   2 tablesps shortening
Sift flour salt & baking powder
into bowl, add the shortening and rub
in very lightly add enough cold
milk to hold together, add the raisins
& mix. Place dough on floured
board, roll or pat with hands until
1 inch thick then cut with
biscuit cutter and brush tops with cold milk
Bake in hot oven 20 to 25 minutes.

These are biscuits in the American sense, similar to a savoury scone, rather than a sweet biscuit in the British sense.

Take the time to chop the raisins. A nuisance, but if left whole they have an annoying habit of popping out of the dough as you work it: the smaller the pieces, the easier they are to mix in.

The original recipe has the amount of milk wrong, which is corrected in our recipe. It is also better to mix in the raisins before rather than after adding the milk to the flour mixture.

RAISIN BISCUITS
makes about 8 biscuits

2 cups (300 g) flour
2 teaspoons (10 g) baking powder
½ teaspoon (3.3 g) salt
2 tablespoons (30 g) shortening

1 cup (150 g) raisins
¾ cup (190 ml) cold milk, plus extra if needed, and more to brush on tops of biscuits

Preheat the oven to 400°F. Lightly grease a baking sheet (or use parchment or a silicone mat). Chop the raisins. Mix the flour, salt, and baking powder. Rub in the shortening until no lumps can be felt. Mix in the chopped raisins and break up any clumps. Add the milk and stir to bring the dough together; add another tablespoon of milk if the mixture does not hold together. Turn out the dough and fold it over 2 or 3 times to spread the raisins evenly throughout the dough. Press or roll the dough to about 1 inch thick. Cut out disks with a 2½-inch cookie cutter. Re-roll the scraps and cut out more disks for a total of 8. Place on the prepared sheets, brush the tops lightly with milk, and bake 25 to 30 minutes, or until the tops are lightly browned. Place on a rack to cool.

130 Washington Apple Pie

1½ cups pastry flour   ⅓ cup shortening
½ teasp salt   ½ teasp baking powder
water, 5 to 6 apples 1 tablesp flour
6 tablesp. sugar   ¼ teasp cinnamon
1 tablesp butter.

Sift together the pastry flour, salt
& b. powder; add the shortening & chop
lightly till well blended. Moisten to
a dough with ice-water adding it
gradually & cutting it with a knife
Divide in halves & place half on
a floured board, roll out deftly
a line a pie-pan. Thoroughly mix
the one tablesp of flour with half
the sugar & sprinkle evenly in the
crust. Fill the pan with the apples
cut in eighths. Mix the rest of the sugar
with the cinnamon & sprinkle
over all. Dot with bits of butter
add one tablesp water. Wet the edges
of the lower crust & cover with the
top crust in which gashes have been
cut. Press the edges down firmly,
sprinkle with cold water & bake
40 mins at 450 °F.

Exactly why this and the following two recipes are called Washington is not clear. There is a Washington pie from America which is really a layered cake (see recipe 26), so these are no relation. Perhaps they were copied from a periodical extolling all things Washingtonian.

The detail of this recipe is quite unlike Mrs. Ayre's other recipes, and seems entirely normal to modern eyes.

The pastry can be fragile, because it has to be rolled thinly to cover a 9-inch pie plate and its rim.

Any apple can be used, but we like the texture and tartness of Granny Smiths in this pie.

The instructions say to cut the apples into eighths, which leaves a lot of wasted space. It is best to start with a layer of one-eighth pieces, then chop other pieces of the apple finely to fill the spaces around the eighths.

The number of apples required depends on their size and the dimensions of the pie plate. If you use large apples (about 8 oz each), you may need only 4, but the best approach is to have surplus apples on hand and simply fill the pie with as many as needed.

WASHINGTON APPLE PIE
makes one 9-inch (23 cm) pie

4 to 6 apples
1 tablespoon (10 g) flour
6 tablespoons (75 g) sugar
¼ teaspoon (0.75 g) cinnamon
1 tablespoon (15 g) butter
1 tablespoon (15 ml) water, plus extra for sprinkling

For the pastry
1½ cups (225 g) flour
⅓ cup (65 g) shortening
½ teaspoon (3.3 g) salt
½ teaspoon (2.5 g) baking powder
4–6 tablespoons (60–90 ml) cold water

For the pastry, mix the flour, salt, and baking powder, then rub or chop in the shortening until no lumps are visible or can be felt. Stir in about 4 tablespoons of cold water, adding 1 or 2 more tablespoons if needed to make the dough hold together. Turn out on a lightly floured surface, knead 2 or 3 times to make everything homogeneous, and divide into halves.

Roll out one half on a lightly floured surface to a circle that will line a 9-inch pie plate, including its rim. Mix half the sugar with the tablespoon of flour and sprinkle evenly over the pastry lining the pie plate.

Preheat the oven to 450°F. Peel, core, and cut 4 apples into 8 pieces lengthways, and place as many as fit neatly in the pie plate. Chop the remaining pieces into small dice and pack them around and over the slices, mounding slightly toward the middle. Peel, core, and chop more apples as needed to fill the pie.

Mix the other half of the sugar with the cinnamon and sprinkle evenly over the apples. Sprinkle a tablespoon of water over it all, letting the water wash some of the sugar and cinnamon down between the apples. Cut the tablespoon of butter into small pieces and scatter over the top.

Roll the other half of the pastry into a circle that will cover the pie. Wet the rim of the bottom layer of pastry and lay on the top layer. Press the rims firmly together to seal, then trim off any surplus pastry. Cut a cross in the centre of the top layer of pastry. Sprinkle about a teaspoon of cold water over the top pastry and bake 35 to 40 minutes, or until the pastry is well browned with dark brown edges. Remove from the oven and serve warm or cold.

131 Washington Salmon Supreme

2 cups freshly cooked or canned salmon
4 tablesp melted butter or margarine
1 ½ teasp salt, ⅓ teasp pepper   1 tablesp minced parsley   3 tablesp chopped celery
4 eggs   ½ cup cracker crumbs
2 cups cooked peas   1 cup milk
½ cup salmon liquor   1 tablesp corn flour
1 tablesp butter   ½ teasp salt
⅛ teasp pepper   1 tablesp catchup

Measure & drain salmon, reserving
Liquor. Remove skin & bones & chop
Fine. Add the melted butter, salt pepper
Parsley & celery. Beat the eggs well
Combine with the cracker crumbs &
add to first mixture. Mix well
pack in buttered mould & steam 1 hour.
Turn out on a hot platter, garnish with
the peas heated and seasoned to taste
& serve with the following sauce: Scald
the milk combine the cornstarch
& salmon liquor and add – stirring well
Then add butter, salt, pepper, & cook
3 mins. Just before serving add
catchup a little at time.

Canned salmon was plentiful in the early 20th century, so we used it here. If you wish to use fresh salmon, poach it gently with about ¼ cup of water, and then

save all the cooking liquid, topped up to ½ cup if necessary with milk.

We know from advertisements that ½-pound and 1-pound cans of salmon were available in Mrs. Ayre's day, but a range of sizes are available now. Use enough to yield 2 cups of drained salmon, with skin and bones removed.

The salt in the original recipe is excessive, so it is reduced in our recipe below.

Ketchup, or "catchup," came in several varieties: tomato, mushroom, and "tobasco" ketchup were all advertised in the St. John's press in the first decades of the 20th century. Which one did she mean? It has to be the tomato, since we think the primary purpose of the ketchup is to colour the sauce in keeping with the salmon (although it does add some flavour), and it is best to add it in small portions until the sauce is to one's liking.

WASHINGTON SALMON SUPREME
serves 6

4 eggs
½ cup (50 g) cracker crumbs
4 tablespoons (60 g) butter or margarine
1 teaspoon (6.5 g) salt
⅓ teaspoon (1 g) pepper

1 tablespoon (4 g) parsley
3 tablespoons (12 g) celery
2 cups (450 g) canned or
 fresh cooked salmon
2 cups (240 g) fresh or frozen peas

For the sauce

1 cup (250 ml) milk
½ cup (125 ml) salmon juice
1 tablespoon (7.5 g) corn flour
1 tablespoon (15 g) butter

½ teaspoon (3.3 g) salt
⅛ teaspoon (0.4 g) pepper
1 tablespoon (15 ml) tomato ketchup
 or more to taste

Heavily grease a 1½-quart pudding basin or other mould. Empty cans of salmon into a small sieve and drain. Reserve the liquid—there should be at least ½ cup; if not, make up to that volume with milk. Remove the skin and bone before measuring and mashing the salmon.

Melt the butter. Chop the celery finely. Beat the eggs, then mix in the crumbs, salt, pepper, parsley, celery, and melted butter. Stir in the mashed salmon. Pack this into the prepared basin, tie a cloth over the top, and steam for 1 hour. Do not let the steamer boil dry; check the water level at about halftime and add boiling water if necessary.

Meanwhile, cook the peas, season to taste, and keep warm.

For the sauce, heat the milk in a small saucepan. Whisk in the corn flour and the reserved ½ cup of salmon liquid, and continue to heat until it thickens. Stir in the 1 tablespoon of butter and the salt and pepper. Add teaspoons of ketchup until the colour and taste of the sauce is right. Keep warm.

When the salmon has steamed, turn it out on a platter and surround with the peas. Serve warm with the sauce passed separately.

132 Washington Apple Sauce Cake

1 cup sugar   ½ cup unsalted shortening
1¼ cup unsweetened apple sauce
2 teasp soda   1¼ teasp salt
1 teasp cinnamon   ½ teasp cloves
½ teasp nutmeg   2 cups pastry flour
¼ cup butter   ½ cup seedless raisins
1 cup powdered sugar   ½ cup chopped walnuts
1 tablesp milk
1 teasp vanilla

Cream the shortening & sugar add apple sauce into which soda has been beaten. The add the flour sifted with the salt & spices, reserving a little to dust over the raisins & nuts, which should be added last. Beat well together & turn into a well-greased and floured shallow cake pan. Bake in a 375 °F oven about 40 minutes. Ice when cold with a butter frosting Made by blending the remaining ingredients.

If you have no ready-made applesauce, make your own: peel, core, and roughly chop 2 large Granny Smith apples, each around 8 ounces, or more smaller ones. Bring to a boil in a small saucepan with 4 tablespoons of water and simmer until they will mash up easily with a spoon or potato masher.

Pastry flour is not necessary but it can be used. We recommend pecans rather than walnuts, because the latter are prone to rancidity.

WASHINGTON APPLESAUCE CAKE
makes one 8-inch (20 cm) cake

- 1 cup (200 g) sugar
- ½ cup (100 g) shortening
- 1¼ teaspoons (8 g) salt
- 1 teaspoon (3 g) cinnamon
- ½ teaspoon (1.5 g) cloves
- ½ teaspoon (1.5 g) nutmeg
- 1¼ cups (315 ml) unsweetened applesauce
- 2 teaspoons (10 g) baking soda
- 2 cups (300 g) flour
- ½ cup (75 g) seedless raisins
- ½ cup (50 g) walnuts or pecans

For the icing
- ¼ cup (55 g) butter
- 1 cup (120 g) icing sugar
- 1 tablespoon (15 ml) milk
- 1 teaspoon (5 ml) vanilla

Preheat the oven to 375°F. Grease and flour an 8-inch cake pan. Chop the nuts coarsely. Cream together the sugar and shortening, then mix in the salt, spices, and the applesauce. Mix the flour with the baking soda and mix in, followed by the raisins and chopped nuts. Pour and scrape into the prepared pan. Bake 45 to 50 minutes, or until a small skewer inserted in the thickest part comes out clean. Turn out on a rack to cool.

For the icing, mash together the ingredients, making sure that all the lumps of butter are incorporated.

When the cake is cool, spread the icing over the top of it.

133 Boiled Prune Cake

1½ cups dried prunes
½ cup melted shortening
¾ cup sugar
1 egg yolk
½ cup prune juice
1 ¾ cups pastry flour
1 teasp soda
1 teasp cinnamon
½ " nutmeg
1 egg white
1 teasp vanilla
½ teasp salt

Wash prunes. Soak over night cold water pit and cut to raisin size. Cover boiling water cook until tender. Cream together the sugar and melted shortening Add egg-yolk, slightly beaten. Sift together the dry ingredients & add to the mixture alternately with the prune juice. Then add prune pulp vanilla & last the egg-white beaten stiff   pour into a greased and floured pan Bake at 325 °F for 1¼ hrs.

Even though today's prunes are probably not as dry as those in Mrs. Ayre's day, it is still useful to give them a preliminary soak to make the pits easy to remove and to ensure they cook quickly. Chopping them to the size of raisins is a guessing game, because after soaking they are so soft it is difficult to see how big any particular piece is, so just chop them until there are no obviously large pieces left. Be careful when trying to simmer the soaked and chopped prunes: because they are so mushy, it is like boiling applesauce—unless you are very careful, it splatters all over the place.

Melting the shortening is not strictly necessary, although before mechanical beaters it did help to disperse the fat quickly into the sugar.

An unpromising name, but this is an excellent cake, and well worth making.

BOILED PRUNE CAKE
makes one 8-inch (20 cm) cake

1½ cups (250 g) prunes with pits
½ cup (125 ml) boiling water
½ cup (100 g) shortening
¾ cup (150 g) sugar
1 egg
1 teaspoon (3 g) cinnamon
½ teaspoon (1.5 g) nutmeg
1 teaspoon (5 ml) vanilla
½ teaspoon (3.3 g) salt
1¾ cups (265 g) flour
1 teaspoon (5 g) baking soda
½ cup (125 ml) prune juice

Soak the prunes overnight in excess cold water. Preheat the oven to 325°F. Grease and flour an 8-inch cake pan. Remove the pits from the prunes. Chop the prunes coarsely to about the size of raisins. Place in a small saucepan, add the boiling water, bring to a boil, and simmer for 3 or 4 minutes, or until completely mushy. Set aside off the heat.

Separate the egg. Melt the shortening and cream with the sugar. Mix in the egg yolk, cinnamon, nutmeg, salt, and vanilla. Mix the flour and baking soda, then beat into the sugar mixture alternately with the prune juice. Stir in the boiled prune pulp. Whip the egg white to stiff peaks and fold into the mixture. Pour and scrape into the prepared pan. Bake 60 to 65 minutes, or until a small skewer inserted in the thickest part comes out clean.

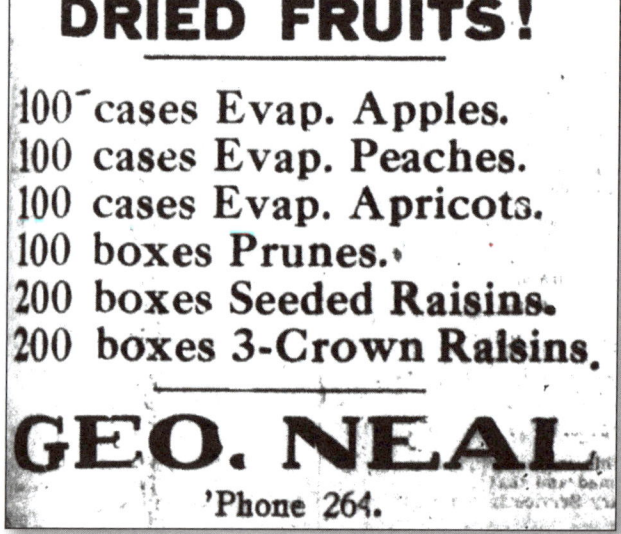

Evening Telegram, December 12, 1918.

134 Chowder. Mrs H. Head makes best chowder

Boil fish and bones
Fry out fat pork. Slice 2 small onions
& fry 3 mins - add 3 or 4 potatoes
sliced. Cover with water when done
add fish flakes and liquor then
a pint milk and lastly thicken with
2 tablesp flour mixed with milk
add little butter.

Mrs. H. was perfectly correct: codfish heads do indeed make the best chowder. That mass of bone and connective tissue yields a wonderful broth after gentle simmering. In fact, it is better to simmer the head and bones first, rather than with the flesh of the fish, which can get overcooked. Our version has tweaked Mrs. H.'s instructions, while staying true to her principles.

The cubes of fat pork (or bacon) are fried until the fat has rendered and the cubes are crisp and shrunken. These are scrunchions. Scoop them out and reserve for another use, or sprinkle a few on each serving of chowder. This is not mentioned in the original recipe, but a perfectly ordinary practice both then and now.

The liquor in the original recipe we call broth in our version below.

CHOWDER Mrs. H.
serves 6 to 8

- 1 small (about 1.25 kg) codfish, gutted, head on
- 1 quart (1 l) water
- ½ cup (80 g) fatback pork or fatty bacon
- 2 small (about 100 g each, untrimmed weight) onions
- 4 medium (about 150 g each, untrimmed weight) potatoes
- 1½ teaspoons (10 g) salt
- 2 cups (500 ml) milk
- 2 tablespoons (30 g) butter
- 2 tablespoons (20 g) flour

Remove the fillets from the fish and the skin from the fillets. Put the head, bones, skin, and scraps into a 4-quart saucepan, add the water, bring to a boil, and simmer on very low heat for about 30 minutes. Strain off the broth and reserve; discard the solids.

Meanwhile, chop the fatback pork or bacon into ¼-inch cubes and fry gently in a 4-quart saucepan until the fat has rendered and the cubes are crisp and shrunken. Remove and reserve these scrunchions.

Peel and chop the onions coarsely and fry gently until soft and translucent in the fat remaining in the saucepan. Add the reserved fish broth. Add the peeled potatoes cut in ¾-inch cubes and about 1 teaspoon of the salt. Bring to a boil and simmer about 10 minutes or until the potatoes are nearly cooked.

While the potatoes are simmering, melt the butter in a 2-quart saucepan, stir in the flour to make a smooth paste, add the milk and the rest of the salt, then bring to a boil, stirring frequently, and simmer for 5 minutes.

When the potatoes are nearly cooked, add the thickened milk and simmer another 5 minutes. Cut the reserved fillets into 1-inch chunks and add to the pot. Simmer on a very low heat about another 10 minutes or until the chunks of fish start to fall apart. Serve hot, with a few of the reserved scrunchions on top of each bowl of chowder if desired.

135 Cod fish.

Sterilize Bottles. Par-boil fish in fish boiler. Put fish in bottles Cover with par-boiled water. Cook 3 hours boiling all time.

This recipe in its existing form is potentially deadly. Do not attempt it unless you have specialized knowledge and equipment; see the general notes about bottling (recipe 71). There is absolutely no point in parboiling the cod before putting into jars because it will get more than enough cooking in the processing, and for the same reason there is no point using parboiled water.

CODFISH (bottled)
fills four 2-cup (500 ml) Mason jars

8 cups (about 2 kg, trimmed weight) cod fillet

1 teaspoon (6.5 g) salt

Cube the fish and pack into jars, leaving about 1½ inches of headroom in each. Put about ¼ teaspoon of salt in each jar, put on lids and rings, and process in a pressure cooker.

Pickavance & Murphy

136 Shrimp Chowder.

Fry out in kettle ¼ cup diced fat pork. Remove crispy bits & in the fat cook 1 lg onion chopped When onion is yellow - do not let it burn - add 1 cup of celery cut in ½ inch pieces & 1 qt boiling water. Cook 15 minutes longer & add 1 pt milk When this again comes to boil, thicken slightly then add 1 qt diced potatoes 2 teasp salt, ¼ teasp pepper & ½ teasp celery salt. Let all come to a boil and add 2 cups raw shrimps shelled & prepared for cooking. Cook 15 mins longer and add 1 pt milk. When this again comes to a boil, thicken slightly with 1 tablesp each flour and butter cooked together. Pour into serving dishes & sprinkle with paprika or finely minced parsley. This way as main dish. Make thinner soup.

The fat pork is more usually known as fatback, slabs of salted pork fat often used in the Newfoundland kitchen. Frying out the diced fatback is both rendering fat for subsequent cooking and making "crispy bits" (scrunchions). The implication is that the crispy bits are discarded, but many people would have sprinkled these on the finished dish. Bacon can be used instead—as fatty as possible and preferably unsmoked, although that is a rarity. If using leaner bacon, add a tablespoon of lard or oil so that there is something to cook the onions in.

We used small (135–145 per lb), wild-caught Newfoundland shrimp, pre-cooked and frozen. With no need for any cooking, our recipe below has been adjusted accordingly.

This makes a substantial main course, but as the recipe indicates, it can also become a soup by adding extra milk: 2 more cups would make soup for 8 or more.

SHRIMP CHOWDER
serves 4 to 6

- ¼ cup (40 g) fatback
- 1 large (250 g, untrimmed weight) onion
- 1 cup (125 g) celery
- 1 quart (1 l) boiling water
- 4 cups (650 g, trimmed weight) potato
- 2 teaspoons (13 g) salt
- ¼ teaspoon (0.75 g) pepper
- ½ teaspoon (3.3 g) celery salt
- 2 cups (225 g) small shrimp
- 1 pint (500 ml) milk
- 1 tablespoon (10 g) flour
- 1 tablespoon (15 g) butter
- paprika or chopped parsley for garnish

Chop the fatback into ¼-inch dice and fry in a 4-quart saucepan on a low heat until the fat has rendered and the scrunchions are pale brown. Remove the scrunchions and reserve. Peel and chop the onion and fry on a low heat in the rendered fat until soft and translucent. Chop the celery into ½-inch dice and mix with the onions. Add the boiling water, bring back to a boil, and simmer about 15 minutes.

Cut the peeled potato into ¾-inch cubes. Add the potato, salt, pepper, and celery salt to the saucepan. Bring it back to a boil, then simmer about 15 minutes, or until the potatoes are just cooked.

In a separate small saucepan, melt the butter. Mix in the flour, then the milk, bring just to a boil, whisking frequently, and simmer about 5 minutes.

When the potato is cooked, mix in the milk mixture and the shrimp, bring back to a boil, and simmer for about 1 minute, just to heat the shrimp. Ladle into individual soup dishes and garnish to taste.

137 Sauce Tartare.

Add chopped pickles olives capers and parsley to thick mayonaise dressing.

A good tartare sauce is completely different from the insipid commercial versions. It should be based on a good homemade mayonnaise, and is far inferior made with commercial mayonnaise, so do not be tempted. Good with all sorts of cold fish, shellfish, and poultry.

The inclusions are a matter of personal taste but basically should be an assortment of vinegary, savoury, salty ingredients in small pieces. This combination follows Mrs. Ayre's suggestions but is only one of multiple possibilities, so leave out any ingredient not to your liking and add things that are.

SAUCE TARTARE
makes about ¾ cup (190 ml)

- ½ cup (125 ml) thick mayonnaise, homemade
- 4 small (each about 35 g) gherkins in vinegar (not sweet gherkins)
- 16 (35 g) stuffed Manzanilla olives
- 2 tablespoons (20 g) capers
- 2 tablespoons (8 g) parsley

Coarsely chop the gherkins, olives, and capers. Finely chop the parsley. Combine all ingredients.

Shrimps canned. Remove from liquor & drain Remove intestinal vein before used.

138 Shrimp Stew.

Creamed shrimps on crackers toast or pastry shells.

Fried shrimps like oysters egg + bread crumbs.

Sauce Tartare.

Scalloped shrimps cracker crumbs + sauce like salmon.

The note on canned shrimp clearly refers to recipe 138, which is simply a list of suggestions for what to do with shrimp.

Canned shrimp were usually the only ones available in the Newfoundland of Mrs. Ayre's day. Fortunately, canned shrimp have been almost entirely eclipsed by frozen ones these days, to the point where the former can be hard to find, and those that can be found are firmly in the disgusting category: to be avoided. But frozen or canned, her advice to remove the intestinal vein (a dark line running down the convex side of the shrimp) is sound, although mostly it has been removed from frozen shrimp in their processing.

SHRIMP STEW

This probably refers to something like recipe 136, which is a stew by another name. Creamed dishes simply meant vegetables, fish, or meat dressed with a white sauce, a béchamel (see recipe 61). Small Newfoundland shrimp suit this dish better than larger ones.

CREAMED SHRIMPS ON TOAST
serves 6

4 cups (450 g) small, cooked, peeled Newfoundland shrimp
1 cup (250 ml) white (béchamel) sauce

6 slices bread
butter for toast

Toast the slices of bread, butter them, and keep warm. Gently warm the sauce if it is cold. Stir in the shrimp and heat through. As soon as the mixture is warm, it is ready to use because the shrimp are already cooked. If using uncooked shrimp, very gently simmer the mixture for 2 or 3 minutes until the shrimp are cooked.

When the shrimp and sauce are warmed through or cooked, divide them between the slices of buttered toast.

For fried shrimp we used medium sized (about 50–60 per lb), because breading and frying the small Newfoundland shrimp is far too fiddly. The crumbs are better if they are fresh and moist.

FRIED SHRIMP
serves 4 as a light meal

1 pound (450 g, about 55 shrimp) medium shrimp
2 eggs
2 pinches (0.2 g) salt
1½ cups (120 g) fresh bread crumbs
oil or lard for frying

Remove any shells and dorsal vein from the shrimp. Blot dry with a cloth or paper towel. Beat the egg with the salt. Spread the bread crumbs in a wide, shallow pan. Stir the dried shrimp around in the beaten egg, transfer to a sieve, and let the excess egg drain off.

Dump the shrimp into the pan of bread crumbs and toss to coat. Lift them out, shake off the surplus crumbs, and set aside in another pan. Put enough oil or lard in a heavy frying pan to make a layer about ⅛ inch (3 mm) deep and put on a medium heat. When the oil or lard is hot (rippling on the surface), quickly put in the shrimp and fry for about 2 minutes until browned on one side; flip over and brown the other side. Fry in as many batches as necessary. Remove and place on a clean cloth or paper towel to drain the excess fat. Serve while hot.

SHRIMPS WITH TARTARE SAUCE
makes 4 appetizer servings

2 cups (225 g) small, cooked, peeled Newfoundland shrimp

½ cup (125 ml) tartare sauce (recipe 137)

Blot the shrimp dry and mix with the tartare sauce. Divide between 4 serving cups.
For scalloped shrimp we took clues from elsewhere in the recipe collection (e.g., recipe 61) and came up with what she may have meant by this. We used an oval pie dish, about 6 by 8 inches at the widest, but any baking dish can be used.

SCALLOPED SHRIMPS
serves 4 to 6

1 pound (450 g, about 55 shrimp) medium shrimp
1½ cups (375 ml) white (béchamel) sauce

1 cup (100 g) cracker or bread crumbs
2 tablespoons (30 g) butter

Preheat the oven to 350°F. Mix the sauce with the shrimp and spread the mixture evenly in a baking dish. Melt the butter and toss with the crumbs. Spread the buttered crumbs evenly over the top of the shrimp and sauce. Bake 45 to 55 minutes, or until the crumbs are well browned and the sauce has bubbled through in several places. Serve hot.

139 Brawn

*Take a hock well meated & chopped
Wash well and place in a large
Boiler cover well with cold water and
Boil about 2½ hours then take out
The bones & cut off the meat
Returning the bones to the stock and
Boil till the bones are clean & white
This will take at least another 2½ or
3 hours take out and skim off all the
fat from the stock & put in the
meat which has been minced
with a little well chopped onion
savory pepper & salt return to the
fire & boil or simmer till it jells
When you think it has boiled
enough try a little in cold place
to harden. Put in mould and leave
all night.*

Brawn is more usually made from the head of an animal, but any part which has a lot of bone and connective tissue in proportion to potentially tough meat can be used. All mammals have hocks, but when used alone in a kitchen context this usually meant a pork hock, which is what we used here. Buy as large a hock as possible—over 2 pounds at minimum—because the effort is hardly worthwhile for a smaller one, and in fact this recipe is conveniently doubled. If the hock is whole, get the butcher to chop or saw it into four or five pieces.

After the bones and scraps have boiled for the second time, it is much better to chill the liquid and then remove the solid fat, rather than try to skim off the fat as the recipe suggests.

The amount of savory is flexible, and the amount recommended below is probably toward the maximum; it works just as well with half as much. Similarly, the amounts of salt and pepper are toward the maximum, so reduce according to taste, but bear in mind that brawn is served cold, which mutes the tastes of both salt and pepper.

The recipe calls for checking to see if the liquid will jell, but there is absolutely no need for this when using a pork hock because by the time it has finished simmering it is guaranteed to set to a stiff jelly.

BRAWN
serves 4 to 6

1 pork hock, at least 2¼ pounds (1 kg)
2 quarts (2 l) water
1 medium (150 g, untrimmed weight) onion
1 tablespoon (3 g) savory
¾ teaspoon (5 g) salt
½ teaspoon (1.5 g) pepper

Put the cut-up hock into a 4-quart saucepan with the water. Bring to a boil, skim off the bulk of the foam, and simmer for 2½ hours.

Lift the pieces from the saucepan, and when cool enough to handle, separate all the meat and reserve. Return the skin, fat, and bones to the saucepan and simmer another 3 hours. Strain and discard the solids. Chill the liquid and scrape off the solidified fat (or skim off the liquid fat if you are in a hurry).

Bring the de-fatted liquid back to a boil. Finely chop the onion and add to the pot, then simmer about 15 minutes or more until the onion is soft. Chop the reserved meat coarsely and add to the pot with the savory, salt, and pepper. Continue to simmer until the mixture is reduced to about 2 cups. Pour into a 3-cup mould or loaf pan and chill. Turn out onto a plate and serve in slices.

140 Meat Loaf

> 2 lbs beef steak   8 soda biscuits
> 1 lb raw ham   rolled fine
> 1 egg to bind & little milk
> Steam 2 hrs put in oven 1 hour

We assume the meats have to be chopped finely, either by hand or through a meat-grinder. Hand chopping gives a superior texture, but the convenience of the grinder usually wins. We have converted Mrs. Ayre's soda crackers into Purity cream crackers and "rolled" (pounded) them fine. Seasoning is needed, which is included in the recipe below.

Finishing the meat loaf in the oven is to attractively brown it. It can be put directly in the oven in the basin or container it was cooked in (be sure to take off the cloth), but it is better turned out, to expose more surface for browning. We suspect this is what the recipe intended and what we recommend below. Be careful when turning it out; there will be a quantity of accumulated juices which can splash about.

MEAT LOAF
serves 6 to 8

2 pounds (900 g, trimmed weight) beef
1 pound (450 g) raw ham
5 (50 g each) cream crackers
1 egg
½ cup (125 ml) milk
1½ teaspoons (10 g) salt
½ teaspoon (1.5 g) pepper

Grease a 3-quart pudding basin, loaf pan, or other similar container. Grind (or chop by hand) the beef and the ham. Smash the crackers into fine crumbs. Mix the crumbs, egg, salt, pepper, and milk to make a smooth paste. Mix in the ground beef and ham. Put this in the prepared container, tie a cloth over the top, and steam for 2 hours. Do not let the steamer boil dry; check the water level about halfway through and add boiling water as necessary.

Preheat the oven to 350ºF. Turn out the meat loaf and the cooking juices into a baking dish and bake 1 hour, basting 4 or 5 times with the juices in the pan, or until the juices are reduced to a glaze and starting to blacken at the edges so that basting is no longer possible. Serve hot or cold.

Endnotes

Notes from Chapter 2, "Agnes Marion Miller Ayre."

1. Personal communication from Agnes's granddaughter, Agnes Marion Murphy, 2017.

2. Ibid.

3. Ibid.

4. Janet Murphy, "Agnes Marion Ayre," in *Remarkable Women of Newfoundland and Labrador. A Collection of Biographical Sketches Prepared by the St. John's Local Council of Women as a Project to Mark International Women's Year* ([St. John's, NL]: Valhalla Press Canada, 1976), 41–42.

5. A.M. Ayre, "Flowers of Newfoundland," in *The Book of Newfoundland*, ed. J.R. Smallwood (St. John's: Newfoundland Book Publishers, Ltd., 1937), 1:86–103.

6. Ibid.

7. "Current Events Club—Woman Suffrage—Newfoundland Society of Art," *Book of Newfoundland* 1:199–201. This article is unattributed but there seems no doubt from the context and style that it was written by Agnes herself.

8. http://collections.mun.ca/cdm/landingpage/collection/cns_ayre.

9. *Evening Telegram*, St. John's NL, October 10, 1906. School of Art Examination Results.

10. Murphy, "Agnes Marion Ayre"

11. "Current Events Club."

12. Ibid., 201.

13. *Wild Flowers of Newfoundland*, part III (privately published by A.M. Ayre; agents L. Reeve and Co., Ashford, Kent, England, 1935). This is a 213-page, 11.5 by 15-centimetre book in the style of a field guide.

14. Ayre, "Flowers of Newfoundland."

15. http://collections.mun.ca/cdm/landingpage/collection/cns_ayre.

Notes from Chapter 3, "The Notebook."

1. *The Ladies' College Aid Society Cook Book, Arranged from Tried and Proven Recipes* (St. John's, NL: Ladies' College Aid Society of the Methodist Church; Robinson & Currie, Printers and Publishers, 1905).

2. *The Presbyterian Ladies' Aid Cook Book, Arranged from Tried and Proven Recipes* (St. John's, NL: Ladies' Aid Society of St. Andrew's Presbyterian Church; Manning & Rabbitts, Printers and Publishers, 1925).

3. Personal communications from Agnes's granddaughter, Agnes Marion Murphy, 2018.

About the authors

Roger Pickavance was raised in the Welsh Borders, where his lifelong interest in food and cooking started with fruit and vegetables from his parents' garden, trout from local rivers, and Welsh lamb from the hills behind his home. His memories of those tastes are still the benchmarks by which he judges food today. His father was a keen ornithologist, his mother knowledgeable about wild flowers. Their love of the natural world started Roger on the path to a PhD in biology, which in turn led to a faculty position at Memorial University. Now retired, Roger lives, cooks, and writes in St. John's. His first cookbook, *The Traditional Newfoundland Kitchen*, was published in 2017 by Boulder Publications.

Born and raised in St. John's, **Agnes Murphy** attended Bishop Spencer College as had her sister, mother, and grandmother (Agnes Ayre, the inspiration for this cookbook). A graduate of Memorial University and the University of Guelph, Agnes retired in 2017 from a career ini potato breeding research and development with Agriculture and Agri-Food Canada in Fredericton, New Brunswick. While there, Agnes contributed to the release of more than 20 potato cultivars with improved levels of disease and pest resistance, as well as several with brightly pigmented flesh. A long-time Masters swimmer and recreational cyclist, she enjoys the outdoors, reading recipes, and cooking—especially her favourite vegetable, the potato.